Measuring Performance

Measuring Performance

An Easy Guide to Master the Skills of a Researcher

Dennis J. Stevens, Ph.D.

Authors Choice Press
San Jose New York Lincoln Shanghai

Measuring Performance
An Easy Guide to Master the Skills of a Researcher

All Rights Reserved © 2001 by Dennis J. Stevens

Authors Choice Press
an imprint of iUniverse.com, Inc.

For information address:
iUniverse.com, Inc.
5220 S 16th, Ste. 200
Lincoln, NE 68512
www.iuniverse.com

ISBN: 0-595-18466-9

Printed in the United States of America

CONTENTS

LIST OF TABLES

PREFACE

This book should be considered as an easy guide in your journey to develop, understand, and evaluate events in your life, at your workplace, and in your community. Although this work uses a police strategy as a model to test, any model would be appropriate. Some might call this work a how-to book on research methodology. But, it seems to me that this is a quick easy way to learn what you need to know to measure performance with some degree of professionalism without all the unnecessary icons or scholarly fluff. This work is readable by the average person who wants to advance skill levels without taking a stressful university course to do it. Finally, this book does work well for those of us who need to brush up some of our evaluation skills, too. Dennis J. Stevens

ACKNOWLEDGEMENTS

It must be acknowledged that the following individuals took time from their busy schedules to help guide and edit this work: Professors Nina Silverstein, College of Public and Community Services and Xiaogang Deng, Department of Sociology, and Melissa Driscol, University of Massachusetts Boston. However, the final product including its errors belong to the writer.

KEY WORDS

Applied Tests	Outcomes
Cause and Outcome Relationships	Pure Tests
Community Policing Strategies	Replication
Exhaustive Lists	Reliability
Explicit Measurements	Sample
Fixed Measurements	Socially Approved Rhetoric
Mutually Exclusive Lists	Subjective Thoughts
Objective Thoughts	Validity

INTRODUCTION

The purpose of this book is to guide you through the involved process of measuring performance. In no way does this chapter or the author suggest that the "best way" to understand the testing process is contained on these pages. It is not implied nor expected that you will learn all or even the most prolific ways of assessing performance. But, this chapter will prepare you to develop, conduct, and analyze the performance of others at a skilled level yielding professional results. Why measure performance? Because having skills that others don't, makes you more valuable to an organization and to yourself. That is, you become highly competitive in the workplace. Also, possessing a method of developing options of resolving problems aids in offering reliable recommendations that can lead to informed decisions about your workplace, your community, your family, and equally important, your own personal growth. Other answers are shared below.

Something you need to know is that all performance tests are unique. Therefore every test is different. Each test is different because each test relates to a particular group and number of people or sample, has a different method or design to test, and each probably has a different purpose. Also, they're unique because investigators have many of their own ideas, experiences, skill levels, and issues. Therefore, you should look on this chapter as a working draft to help you in a final product. But, there are specific procedures and objectives that are recommended and expected when producing a professional product. This chapter will guide you through the nuances of those procedures and objectives, but let's understand that while each test is different despite the differences in social facts, there is one primary method of reaching professional results. To help you in this process, there are questions throughout this work that require your input denoted by this icon:

There are also sixteen exercises at the back of the chapter that will guide your thinking. In order to better prepare you as an investigator, it is suggested that you address each of those exercises and questions in some way.

WORK OUTLINE

This work offers information about testing performance, and is a "how to" guide on understanding "fixed data" and "how to" develop and conduct an evaluation of perceptions and attitudes. There are three parts to this work: Part I describes both fixed or conventional measures and explicit measures. Part II offers an Introduction, Media Search, and Rationale relevant to a specific test used to measure the attitudes of community members about police outreach through community policing efforts. And finally, Part III recommends five stages when developing, conducting, and finalizing a performance test based on the attitudes of others.

As an example, the writer developed a test to measure community attitudes, especially the attitudes of culturally diverse populations residing in various cities across the United States, but especially Boston. The focus of this test relates to the impact of policing on those populations. The development of this test will be used to illustrate the points that this chapter intends to make to those individuals interested in measuring performance, too. Be mindful that the subject of community attitudes about policing efforts should not to be construed as the most acceptable subject matter nor should it be considered at the exclusion of all other subject matter. In fact, one of the major points that should be clarified is that we all try to measure performance in subject areas that:

- holds your (or your organization's) attention
- we understand and have access to an appropriate sample
- furthers our knowledge about things we really want to know about
- will aid us personally in related matters such as employment, education, and personal endeavors
- has flexibility and is reasonably able to be measured

Another reason police performance was chosen is that most of us have ideas about policing. Also, many of us have heard about community policing initiatives, and want more information about it. Therefore, the work on these pages will aid some of us to see a different side of this very important American institution. One more point. It is not expected that each of us will agree with every idea offered about policing, but that, too, is an important piece of information about the skill you are about acquire.

Evidence is far greater than expertise or opinion: Strength in Numbers.

Documenting positions (linking facts to both the scholarly and popular media) is something experts with a lot of experience do. Offering opinion, on the other hand, is something folks who have a different set of priorities do. You have to decide how you want others to view you—as an expert or an opinionated individual with little to back your viewpoint. Experts usually support their position with a search of the available work conducted by others and a source of individuals (their sample) to test their concerns. They know that there is more than one side to an event or a question and part of their task is to offer to their readers, as many of those different points of view as reasonably possible—or what can be called a critical analysis of the issue to be studied.

PART I: MEASUREMENTS OF PERFORMANCE

Public expectation and official mandates about every aspect of public and private life and organizations are changing—and one thing about those changes is that they are unchanging. Changes are happening more and more and at both a social and an official level. Social change has to do with changes in the demographics of the American population, the mood of the nation, the experiences of personnel, the loss of opportunities, and immigration.

For instance, over the past 30 years, the bulk of legal and illegal immigrants settling in the United States has not been Western Europeans. People from Africa, Asia such as Cambodia, Thailand, Vietnam, China, and India and countries such as Cuba, Dominican Republic, Brazil, Mexico, and Haiti have settled in the U.S. more than people from Western Europe in the past three decades.

Cultural diversity, as well as ethnic differences, compounds quality lifestyles, product demands, and perceptions of safety and public order. Official change occurs at the institutional level according to institutional official mandates and directives. The need for reliable information to help understand those diverse perspectives and to develop those mandates is centered in measuring various variables such as cultural perspectives, supply and demand, police practices and public policy. There are many ways to measure social facts such as trends, practices, and performance including the use of fixed or conventional measurements.

Fixed Measurements

We measure everything from the productivity of factory workers to rates of infectious illness to the endurance of shortstops. When it comes to public safety, the measurement familiar to most of us is whether reported crime is up or down. This type of measurement is called a fixed or a conventional measurement and it might include a day-to-day monitoring by a public or a private agency or organization. Fixed measurements are routinely conducted and used by organizations including human services, corporations, and private and public agencies such as the police. There are other ways to gauge crime and its effects as well as to measure the performance of police who share responsibility for public safety. For example, police agencies traditionally measure:

- **arrests**
- **patrol stops and citations**
- **calls for service**
- **response time (to the scene of a reported crime)**
- **complaints against officers, and/or**
- **dollar amounts of confiscated contraband and property (drugs, weapons, and cash)**

Can you give some explanation as to the importance of each of these fixed measurements of evaluation? These practices are used to determine the level of police service provided by an agency. By making comparisons between different months, we could also get an idea about the effectiveness of a policy. A typical example of how police agencies use fixed tests of performance follows:

15 arrested, $1m in cocaine seized

More than $1 million worth of drugs were seized early yesterday after State Police dismantled two high-level drug organizations following a yearlong undercover investigation, officials said.

At sunrise, State Police assigned to Attorney General Thomas F. Reilly's office executed 30 search warrants in Billerica, Boston, Charlestown, East Boston, Everett, Medford, Quincy, Revere, Salem, Saugus, and Somerville. Fifteen people were arrested on a variety of drug charges.

During their searches, investigators seized approximately 14 pounds of cocaine with an estimated street value of $1 million; 15 luxury vehicles and three high-end motorcycles with fake handicapped plates; $250,000 in cash; several guns; computers; and tools such as scales used to deal drugs. Thousands of dollars worth of Percocet, 20 pounds of marijuana, and other drugs were also seized.

Assistant Attorney General Jerry Leone, chief of the Criminal Investigation Bureau in the attorney general's office, said the raid will help keep drugs off the street.
''We have made a major dent in the illegal drug trade in the area and have taken millions of dollars of drugs off the streets and away from our children,'' Leone said at a news conference. "It's unfortunate that drugs such as Ecstasy are making their way into young people's hands. This is a huge development in child protection."
The Kelleys allegedly sold Sanders the pills for $2.50 to $4 per pill. The pills were then each sold for $8 to $10 on the street. Police determined that the distribution ring earned approximately $100,000 weekly in illegal drug profits.
This story ran on page B2 of the Boston Globe on 8/17/2000.

Can you think of other ways to use the information you learned about seized drugs? The principle mechanism for determining police effectiveness has historically been—counted and measured in fixed numbers because most data (always plural) are easy to collect and because it is easy to understand the results of those measurements and compare them with other variables. Perhaps the Federal Bureau of Investigation's (FBI) Uniform Crime Report reports one of the best examples of nationwide standardization of categorizing crime.[i]

How did it all start? The FBI website explains that in the 1920's, August Vollmer and the International Association of Chiefs of Police (IACP) recognized the potential value in tracking national crime statistics. The Committee on Uniform Crime Records of the IACP developed and initiated this voluntary national data collection effort in 1930 and still continues to advise the FBI on the UCR Program process. During that same year, the IACP was instrumental in gaining Congressional approval that authorized the FBI to serve as the national clearinghouse for statistical information on crime. In June 1966, the National Sheriffs' Association (NSA) established a Committee on Uniform Crime Reporting to serve in an advisory capacity and to encourage sheriffs throughout the country to fully participate in the Program. Since 1930, through the UCR Program, the FBI has collected and compiled data to use in law enforcement administration, operation, and management, as well as to indicate fluctuations in the level of crime in America. Since 1930, the Federal Bureau of Investigation has compiled the Uniform Crime Reports (UCR) to serve as periodic nationwide assessments of reported crimes not available elsewhere in the criminal justice system.

By 1985, there were approximately 17,000 law enforcement agencies contributing reports either directly or through their state reporting programs. Each year, this information is voluntarily reported in four types of files: (1) Offenses Known and Clearances by Arrest, (2) Property Stolen and Recovered, (3) Supplementary Homicide Reports (SHR), and (4) Police Employee (LEOKA) Data. Offenses. Largely known offenses and persons arrested by police departments are limited to data that are reported. The selected offenses are 1) Murder and Nonnegligent Manslaughter, 2) Forcible Rape, 3) Robbery, 4) Aggravated Assault, 5) Burglary, 6) Larceny-Theft, 7) Motor Vehicle Theft, and 8) Arson. These are serious crimes by nature and/or volume.

The Crime Index total is the sum of selected offenses used to gauge fluctuations in the overall volume and rate of crime reported to law enforcement. The offenses included in the Crime Index total are the violent crimes of Murder and Nonnegligent Manslaughter, Forcible Rape, Robbery, and Aggravated Assault, and the property crimes of Burglary, Larceny-theft, and Motor Vehicle Theft. Because they are not consistently available, Arson figures are not included in the Crime Index total. Arson figures are added to the Crime Index total figures to obtain the Modified Crime Index total.

What about where you work, where you would like to work, or maybe school? What method is generally used in a traditional college to measure the success of a student? I think it can be said that most students are after a high grade, aren't they? Although this chapter has no intention of taking issue with grading systems, in what way can you think of that a grade really measures the accomplishment of a student? What accomplishments can be missed if only an A or a B grade is used as a determinant of a student's success? Would we know if a student ever enjoyed or even understood a subject or not by reviewing his or her grade for a course?

Police agencies today are discovering the impact of new ways to test a number of variables. Subsequently, agencies are recognizing that what they do and how well they do it is essentially subjective (from the eyes of an individual) and personal to those who receive their services. Police agencies have used (and appropriately so) fixed data to aid them to obtain resources to further their mission of controlling crime. For instance, Chief Carolyn M. Kusler, Broken Arrow, Oklahoma Police Department reported in the year 2000 that:

> Lack of manpower was a major concern......an aggressive recruitment campaign to bring the department from 74 sworn officers to its authorized strength of 81. One area of concern was the number of calls for service the department received which in 1998 totaled 25,067 and another 41,812 which were initiated by the department for a total of 66,879 calls for one year. Additionally there were 665 domestic violence reports, 9,807 citations, 1,470 arrests, 555 arrest warrants served, and 36 problem solving projects completed....budget process, increasing the number of authorized positions to 87. Further manpower increases were approved in the 1999-2000 budget moving the authorized strength of sworn personnel to 94 (Stevens, 2000, p.32).

Fixed data serve a valuable purpose; yet, resident perceptions about quality of life issues such as fear of crime is genuinely as important as arrest numbers and, therefore, agencies might want to consider fear of crime perceptions if they are concerned with quality police service. Finally, with the concern moving toward police service and police accountability in a democratic society, police executives are discovering that fixed measures fall short in helping to guide community policing and problem-oriented initiatives. In fact, it was the American Bar Association which argued that police agencies should be measured in accordance with their ability to achieve their mission and their priorities (Trojanowicz &

Dixon, 1974, p. 148). Those writers also urged that the police should be measured with the following as a guide:

1. The highest duties of government, and therefore the police, are to safeguard freedom, to preserve life and property, to protect the constitutional rights of citizens and maintain respect for the rule of law by proper enforcement thereof, and to preserve democratic government.

2. Implicit within this duty, the police have the responsibility for maintain that degree of public order which is consistent with freedom and which is essential if our urban and diverse society is to be maintained.

3. In implementing their varied responsibilities, police must provide maximum opportunity, for achieving desired social change by freely available, lawful and orderly means. And,

4. In order to maximize the use of the special authority and ability of the police, it is appropriate for government, in developing objective priorities for police services, to give emphasis to those social and behavior problems which may require the use of force or the use of special investigative abilities which the police possess. Given the awesome authority of the police to use force and the priority that must be given to preserve life, however, government should firmly, establish the principle that the police should be restricted to using the minimum amount of force necessary in responding to any situation.

Knowing an arrest rate, response time, service call statistics, and dollar amounts of confiscated contraband, can certainly be a guide in understanding the activities of a police agency. We can even compare data with other police agencies to give us a better idea about the similarities and the differences in, for instance, arrest rates. Take a glance at the data complied comparing nine police jurisdictions across the United States as shown in Table 1. We can see that there are differences in a number of the categories offered. For instance, jurisdiction 1 which represents (according to the Key) Broken Arrow, Oklahoma and jurisdiction 2 or Camden, New Jersey have similar sized populations (A), but Camden has 386 sworn officers (B) as compared with the 87 employed by Broken Arrow. Yet, according to the total crime index (I), Camden has 3904 crimes as compared to Broken Arrow's 690 crimes. In fact, Table 1-4 shows that Camden has more violent crime as per the index (J) then all the other jurisdictions surveyed. We can learn a lot about a community when comparing fixed data.

What else can be said about community situations as we review the remaining jurisdictions? How would you explain that larger cities such as Columbus, Ohio and Nashville, Tennessee also report differences in the total crime index, yet the number of officers in both jurisdictions is similar?

Table 1

Jurisdiction Demographics

N=9

	1	2	3	4	5*	6	7	8	9
A	81,000	83,546	641,338	113,561	750000	123,086	531,908	250,572	383,921
B	87	386	1,770	317	376	373	1,500	520	642
C	930	216	362	358	NA	330	355	482	598
D	26	1110	3,104	653	87	265	2,583	1,255	1,851
E	18	96	696	84	NA	154	550	201	161
F	0	42	84	11	NA	16	112	21	41
G	77	1164	2,103	359	66	1,086	6,046	3,781	1,664
H	145	1492	7,618	796	733	506	8,173	1,774	6,260
I	690	3904	13,605	1,903	NA	2,027	17,464	7,032	9,970
J	.008	46.7	21.2	16.7	NA	16.4	32.8	28.0	25.9

Key

A = Population, 1999	1 = Broken Arrow, OK
B = Sworn Officers, 1999	2 = Camden, NJ
C = One Officer to Population, 1999	3 = Columbus, OH
D = Robbery, 1997	4 = Fayetteville, NC
E = Rape, 1997	5 = Harris County, TX
F = Homicide, 1997	6 = Lansing, MI
G = Aggravated Assault, 1997	7 = Nashville, TN
H = Motor Vehicle Theft, 1997	8 = St. Petersburg, FL
I = Total Crime Index, 1997	9 = Sacramento, CA
J = Violent Crime per 100K	

- Since Harris County has more than Precinct 4 officers serving the county, any calculations would be misleading.
- Source: Bureau of Justice Statistics, 1999, 1997 (as cited in Stevens (2001). Case Studies in Community Policing.
- Note: 1997 statistics were used because all of the data indicated were consistent to make comparisons and available for those years.

Despite all the fixed data from the nine jurisdictions displayed in Table 1, how would you determine if any of those agencies have reduced the fear of crime and enhanced quality of life standards of their constituents? What could be said about officer morale in Camden versus Fayetteville? Which of those police agencies have safeguarded freedom, preserved life and property, and maintained respect for the rule of law through due process guarantees and methods of social order? Conceptually, we look to the police to preserve democratic safeguards, and yet we have no way of knowing how comfortable the people are who live in those jurisdictions. We can guess from the huge crime problems of Camden, but in other jurisdictions where crime is better controlled, guesses would be just that. Measuring perceptions or explicit testing is relatively new to most organizations including police agencies and requires a different way of thinking about performance.

Explicit Tests

Understanding police performance through arrest rates, response time, service calls, and dollar amounts of confiscated contraband might prove less efficient in revealing how well a police agency has preserved the democratic process and enhanced quality of life issues than other ways of measuring performance. The need to develop efficient ways of testing performance, attitudes, and perceptions in the 21st century is a big issue among public agencies especially police departments (Eck & LaVigne, 1994). For instance:

> The amount of research on law enforcement matters continues to grow, as does the number of police agencies that volunteer to participate in research efforts. However, law enforcement agencies cannot afford to wait for someone else to publish studies or to wait to be asked to participate in research. They must assume the initiative and conduct studies that directly address pressing concerns. Certainly, in the area of police problem solving efforts, it is the agency's obligation to research and analyze the effectiveness of these efforts (p.64).

If we want to develop a community oriented police agency and recognize that community policing turns the delivery of police services upside down by emphasizing crime prevention through problem solving strategies, knowing arrest rates will serve us only in a limited way. If we want to know how well a program or a policy met its goals, it is unlikely that police response time will offer clues about those outcomes. If we want to measure how well an agency's community outreach is working, (how well are we solving the major problems of the community), who best to ask than community members themselves about their impressions of that outreach.

If we had a magic ball, we could look into the future and make more right decisions than wrong decisions. But, we don't have a magic ball. If you were convinced that a magic ball might exist, would you do what's necessary to read tomorrow's news—today?

One way of looking into the future might be to develop a small window to the future that would help you make reasonable decisions about things you need to know. Most of us want to change the:

—things we can change,
and understand the things we can't change

To help accomplish this task, measurement tests as found in an explicit design lend themselves to sound problem solving solutions and recommendations due to the intended nature of those designs. Explicit evaluation refers to observing behavior (directly and indirectly) and testing a claim about a causal relationship (cause and outcome).[ii] Think of it this way, one goal of explicit testing techniques are to enhance predictive abilities about programs, policies, and/or organizational outcomes. A small window giving access to the future does exist and can be found in an explicit test of public service practices. Here's how it works.

Thinking about Causal Conditions that Can Change Outcomes

When you're thinking about examining performance, you might want to link a set of ideas that help shape your knowledge of the subject. That is, you could say that this is another way of thinking about that performance and the outcome produced by that performance. Our ideas can gain power from built-in logical uniformity and are tested by how well they describe those performances or practices and how well they can help us see the future. "If this happens—then we can expect that outcome," sort of reasoning. For instance, if we think residents comply less often with alcohol laws when there is a full moon, we must ask, "Why?" Is it because the light from full moon makes it possible for those interested in compliance to feel differently about the night when the moon is full over their shoulder?

If so, then test the causal condition (a full moon) against the expected outcome (lack of compliance) to see if there is any predictive value present. See if when the moon is full, what happens to arrest rates among alcohol abusers. It goes up might be a good guess. Ask questions of known drinkers. Observe activities of drinkers at nightclubs and at sporting events on those nights when the moon is full. Compare your results with results from nights when the moon isn't full. If your evidence supports the idea that on a full moon night, people do not comply with liquor laws, than we need to create a way to make the moon less full every night of the week. Let's review what we've covered so far:

- **Causal Condition: Full Moon**
- **Outcome: Less Compliance Towards Liquor Laws when Moon is Full**
- **Predictive Value: When Moon is Full, People Drink More**
- **Recommendation: Make the Moon Less Fuller More Often**

I hope you can see this idea although fun, is not necessarily worth your time since you can't do much about the moon, at least at this time. For right now, we need to know that a complete lunar idea or theory about alcohol compliance would contain specific propositions or ideas about the causal nature of the event. In other words, a good question to examine provides a complete understanding (all sides) of an issue. Your idea will stand even with continued scrutiny, if it is logical and realistic. Of course, your idea can provide a degree of understanding, but it must still be tested to determine how strongly related it is to the causal condition. A good idea to measure, therefore, is a well connected group of assumptions, propositions, and definitions linked in such a way so as to explain and predict outcomes based on the causal condition or said another way—the relationship between two or more variables (Champion, 1993).

 Identify an idea that you want to examine. Break your idea down and identify both the causal condition and your expected outcome.

Causal Facts and Outcomes

Let's get to business. At the community meetings, we learned that juvenile crime in the community is on the rise and that something should be done about it. If behavior is anything like we expect, we might argue that there is always more than one cause for every outcome. Said another way, there are many reasons why juveniles engage in crime. To help build your rationale, let's try a small quiz. Identify five reasons why juveniles commit crime, especially violent crime.

1. _____
2. _____
3. _____
4. _____
5. _____

Now, tell us which idea of yours contributes most toward juvenile violent crime?

_____

Your choice might be a good choice. One purpose of a study is to discover which of your five reasons contributes most to juvenile violent crime. Ask yourself, in what way is my idea logical and reasonable? For the sake of argument, let's say you decide that neglect is a causal factor leading to juvenile crime. That is, by leaving a juvenile alone or unsupervised allows opportunity to engage in a crime of violence. That sounds reasonable, doesn't it?

Exhaustive and Mutually Exclusive

Conceptually, however, neglect can be seen in a number of ways since it can mean different things to different people. When you define the concept of neglect, you are specifying its attributes or what can be called operationalizing it. That is to say that neglect is a conceptual variable that can possess the attributes of "leaving a juvenile alone." Does this attribute of neglect tell the whole story? We need to know that every variable has two important qualities. Its attributes should be:

❖ **exhaustive**

❖ **mutually exclusive**

Exhaustive says that if the variable is to have any utility at measuring performance, you should be able to classify every observation (neglect) in terms of one of the attributes composing the variable. We would be in trouble if we conceptualized neglect strictly in terms of the physical attributes of abandonment. Isn't it true that neglect could include an emotional side, too? Attributes such as rejection, denial of love, and a lack of a sense of belonging could lead to some pretty strange behavior? You can make your list exhaustive my adding other attributes to your list. That is, neglect through child abandonment might produce an opportunity for a youth to engage in criminal activity, yet abandonment might also produce other factors leading to a juvenile to commit a crime of violence.

At the same time, attributes composing a variable must be mutually exclusive. Neglect can mean more than abandonment. Even when a juvenile is in the company of her parent/s every day except for school, in what way could she be neglected? If parent/s drank too much or fought all the time with each other (even if the parents lived apart), couldn't those continued patterns of behavior give rise to neglect, too? That is, we should develop attributes of neglect in such a way that it is a product of parental behavior including abandonment and continued inappropriate behavior such as parental drunkenness and quarreling. In this case, attributes should be defined more precisely by specifying "neglect" as meaning more than juvenile abandonment—neglect can be both physical and emotional.

> **Attributes composing any variable must be exhaustive and mutually exclusive.**

With that said, let's test our idea about neglect leading youths to crimes of violence. First, develop a question to investigate such as: is neglect one path to juvenile crimes of violence? Next, test your idea.

Test It

Your hunch is that neglect among juveniles gives rise to violent crime. You now need to develop a way to investigate it. If your test is valid, then you should be able to see a little into the future—see predictions and make recommendations about parental behavior and juveniles and crime. You could as a parent, a police officer, or a school teacher change (some) expected outcomes (crime) by managing the causal issue—parental behavior.

Drawing on an earlier study, it was revealed that when parents quarreled all of the time with each other, one product of parental fighting led to the neglect of their children. In turn, that neglect produced three things:

1.) **the social values of immediate gratification**
2.) **a loss of self control become acceptable and internalized values to process**
3.) **it gave juveniles an opportunity to engage in crime**

That is, when violent offenders incarcerated in a high custody penitentiary (Attica in New York) recalled their early childhood experiences, those experiences remembered most often were that their parents were engaged in a daily struggle with each other (Stevens, 1997). Based on that study, we could argue that supervision or lack of it, is one cause of juvenile crime—the outcome. Once our test is complete and our results support (or don't support) our question, we could report back to the community with our recommendations. For instance, if we conducted the above test or one similar and discovered similar findings (or replication—something that must be "doable" with all studies) we could present those findings to the community and ask their thoughts? What might come from our presentation is that supervising juveniles in after-school program such as those that help students with their homework, might reduce the opportunity of criminal activity among some juveniles and at the same time produce productive individuals. I think this type of recommendation is possible, unlike our full moon idea. There! You have made a prediction—a prediction grounded in some logical fact. It makes sence, doesn't it?

In sum, once you have developed an idea you want to test, and think that that condition might change an outcome, you could say that the cause is "constant" (assume it doesn't change for the sake of your study). The outcome would change once you alter that "constant" or causal effect. That is, once we start and continue homework sessions among juveniles, it is expected that inappropriate conduct will be reduced among that group. If we continue homework sessions, and increase the frequency of those sessions, what might be another prediction we could make?

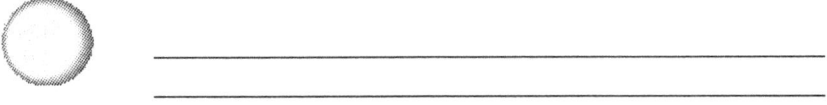

Review of Causal Facts and Outcomes

Let's return to the full moon idea. The full moon can be called a causal factor since it influences or changes something else. That something else is conformity to liquor laws and in this case, that idea is an expected outcome of the full moon effect.

Causal variables are those things that change outcomes.[iii] The outcome has been changed by something independent of itself. If we exercise some control over a causal event for example, could we produce a desired outcome? As with our juvenile neglect question, we can see that one cause of juvenile crime is a lack of supervision. If we supervise juveniles more often what should happen to criminal activities among those juveniles? Right…remember: for every action there is a reaction.

As our thoughts turn to the work of this writer, what is offered is an investigation beginning with a question to examine a belief followed by a definition of the key concepts:

> **Do cultural diverse community members engage in police decision-making processes? My idea is that the more community members, especially culturally diverse members, influence the decisions of the police, the greater the likelihood that public order will be enhanced. Public order includes improving quality of life experiences for its community members. One mission of quality of life experiences is a reduction in both the fear of crime and crime itself. Influencing decisions of the police includes defining social order and police practices. Social order refers to a law abiding community. Police practices refer to police deployment, limits on use of force and pursuits, police priorities, and police personnel training, promotion, and disciplinary action.**

Can you identify the causal factor in the above statement? How about the outcome I'm expecting? If the evidence supports my idea, then describe the expected recommendation that can be made? If the test doesn't support my idea, in what way would the recommendation be different?

Let's try a little quiz. Of the following items, which one of them can change public order relative to a reduction in the fear of crime and enhancement in quality of life experiences for community members?

a. more federal money to hire more officers

b. less federal involvement with local police agencies

c. community involvement in crime

d. community influencing police decisions

If you chose (d.) you're correct. Good job! If we exercise some form of control by successfully implementing a community policing philosophy that includes community decision-making influences in police policy, we can expect or predict that, if all things are equal, the community's life experiences will change and crime will be better controlled. Therefore, knowing which social facts can change an outcome can be a powerful tool in bringing about whatever outcome we're after. In a sense, think about Pavlov's dogs that salivated when they heard a bell ringing linking that bell with food—that is a what we're trying to do. For every action, they is a reaction.

You're right if you think that the same is true if you tip my belief or any cause and outcome, upside-down. That is, the more a police agency moves away from a community policing philosophy, the less residents will feel safe. The social facts changed, didn't they? Develop your own testable question. Identify your causal variable/s (there's always more than one cause for every outcome—remember the number of causes you listed for juvenile crime?). Now, identify what outcome you're looking for. Supposedly, at least until we test it, as your causal effects your expected outcome, does change occur? Have the facts changed? Will your causal question work in reverse? Now that we have a better handle on what we are testing (and this probably is the hardest part of testing performance), we need a brief understanding about facts—social facts.

Social Facts

Equally important, facts such as crime, policing techniques, and community demographics have many antecedent social explanations, as Emile

Durkheim (1933, 1984) once postulated. That is, while there is usually more than one cause for every outcome or affect as discussed above, but what we didn't discuss is that each cause relates to the social environment or social experience more often than other factors (Kruttschnitt, Ward, & Sheble, 1987). Specifically, a police strategy should be seen as strictly an administrative dictate. Rather a social fact suggests that there is more than one cause for every outcome, and therefore suggests that a police strategy is the result of historical, demographic, economic, and political changes found among both a police agency and the constitutes they serve. Social facts vary from community to community even within the same police district. For instance, in the Dorchester district of Boston, there are several distinctive neighborhoods each with its own cultural base and ethnicity including language, customs, and ideals. Community policing initiatives that work well in the Vietnamese community of Dorchester might not work as well as in the Haitian neighborhood of Dorchester. Question: would their idea of public order be different? Do residents who possess primarily a Vietnamese cultural perspective see public order and lifestyles as different than Haitians?

Community policing strategies can also be seen as a result or as a response to a growing and openly competitive drug market and the flight of small commercial establishments from the inner city. Then, too, community policing can be the result of a method for the police to increase arrest rates through community identification of offenders. There are a number of ideas for community policing including some that weren't mentioned, but while each cause contributes differently to the result, they are all linked to the social environment. Therefore, each of these "antecedent" facts (to community policing initiatives) can be best explained largely through a rationale or social framework, as shown above by explaining what is meant by police decisions and so on. It also suggests that the need to measure each and every community in order to get their input should we wish to ultimately control crime, and controlling crime means more arrests, but it also means prevention and responsibility through policing leadership.

Common Sense

Caution needs to be exercised because the subject matter of communities, policing, and crime are familiar to most of us. We could easily move down an awkward path when we try to explain things in our community if we accept common sense ideas and the reasons to support those ideas. Some of our personal beliefs, although logical in our mind, might not be congruent with the facts. Measuring performance along professional standards recommended in this work, helps you better understand the many forces influencing outcomes. It helps you grasp how the whole system operates, and how it's held together. You're not the only one who relies on common scene. For instance, many police agencies are under the impression that all they have to do to change behavior forever is to make a presentation to community and school groups about the consequences of drug abuse. How often do we see the world the way we want it to be instead of the way it is? Many of us are idealists and there isn't anything wrong with that unless we're tinkering with someone else's life. Do we see social facts ideally, too? How many other common sense explanations can you think of that might be questionable in the real world?

What is relevant here is that society is always changing. Would it be in the best interest of the community or the police to have every group with similar decision-making prerogatives? Things are more complex and different than they first appear, and a true understanding comes from looking under the surface for the underlying realities and outcomes.

The process of looking under the surface of the "taken-for-granted" part of social experience has been referred to as debunking myths, argued Peter L. Berger (1963). More specifically, this process is an "unmasking" of different levels of reality. The frame of reference, with "its built-in procedure," said Berger (p.38), "of looking for levels of reality other than those given in the official interpretations of society, carries with it a logical imperative to unmask the pretensions and the propaganda" by which individuals conceal their actions with each other. Do police and community members conceal some of their activities from others? In some cases, it might be appropriate to do so. Can you think of any activity the police should keep a secret? Are there things in the community that should be kept from the police? What role does the First Amendment play in your thoughts?

Also, certain behaviors might be defined one way by one group, and similar behavior might be defined another way by another group. For example, the police could define social disorder differently then the community. In Dorchester, Massachusetts how close might the definitions be between the social problems of the Vietnamese residents and the Haitian residents? Nonetheless, a process of unmasking or debunking is an objective. At the core of this idea is the thought that it is better to be conscious than uncon-scious, and consciousness is a condition of freedom (Burger, 1963). For example, two principle findings from different investigators in the last few decades are that much of the conventional wisdom about organizations is not always correct. One finding suggests that some employees could perform at 35% or less of their work capabilities without being fired for lack of performance. The other principle debunks the idea that an organization that is tightly controlled from the top down works best: "Take up the slack, cut out the fat, get everyone in step, streamline the goals, and the result is success, vitality, profits." Yet, research has found that "decentralized and loosely controlled organizations are often better at adapting, or that slack, foolishness, and some insubordination often provide new ideas and innovations."[iv]

Therefore, in order for community policing to deliver quality police service (depending on the size of the agency, its resources, and the community), working hard and working smart are two different things. Command needs to decentralize both its command post by establishing mini-stations and its hierarchy-of-command by empowering officers and community members with decision-making prerogatives should they wish to help solve community problems. Of course, leadership skills might make a difference in the outcome depending on the professional level of the leadership skills utilized by those commanders (Skogan, 1990; Stevens, 2001b).

One aim of this chapter is to deliver a rationale of community and community policing of which there are many competing definitions. Another aim is to link those rationales with issues concerning the nature of policing and public safety and the subsequent definition of justice in an attempt to understand policing outreach outcomes. We have to see all sides of a question and those sides must be free from our ideal perspectives or bias. It takes, in effect, a critical perspective to produce a professional product. Do you think you can evaluate the conduct of others without drawing on your own personal experience or ideas about that conduct? In fact, one of the prerequisites to a professional study is to do just that. Yet, it is not as easy as it sounds.

Above, we talked about an idea and described it in the use of community members as complying less often with liquor laws when the moon is full. We can make a prediction, after all the evidence is in, which is that the fuller the moon, the lesser the possibility that individuals would conform toward liquor laws. So our goal is to look to the future, but the first step is to develop a causal question to test. That is, a causal question shows that a relationship exists between two or more variables—a causal condition and an outcome.[v]

Next, we might develop a complete lunar explanation or rationale about conformity that would probably describe the various characteristics of conformity and liquor laws. What do we gain by spending some time with a lunar theory? Public agencies need the results from a practical performance test to further goals. In what way might reaching into the lunar future aid community policing strategies? If we say we haven't a strong clue, maybe we need to a test something else, something that has a use—an application. Anything we test should stand up to the question of how can it be applied.

Applied Tests versus Pure Tests

It should be clear that measuring performance of any type should generally have a specific use or application. There are tests that have limited use referred to as pure tests. Often pure tests are conducted for the sake of undertaking an evaluation. For instance, measuring the extent of a police officer culture would seem to offer few rewards once the work was conducted unless we had a reason to examine police culture. If through your test you've discovered a police culture exists, then a logical question might be, now what? There might be a way to turn your findings into something useful, but for now, it might be more resourceful to test useful questions.

The most challenging test for organizations is called an "applied" test. That is, an explicit method of testing performance designed and conducted with a practical use in mind. It is working toward some practical goal. We should begin an explicit test with a question: are bike patrols effective against young gangs? Does reinvestment of school resource officer programs to mentor type programs reduce criminal activities of juveniles? Can empowering community leaders aid public safety? What question do you have that might call for a test of an applied nature in a cause and outcome relationship? A word to the wise: the cause has to be present before the effect. That is, a cause is antecedent (in time) to the outcome. A crime of violence hopefully ends in an arrest, prosecution, and sentencing as opposed to the other way around.

There is an applied test and a pure test of explicit measurement, but most of the time, an applied test would seem to be more valuable to a public agency than a pure test.

PART II: INTRODUCTION: COMMUNITIES AND COMMUNITY POLICING[VI]

Once we accept the idea that a public agency operates in a larger social, economic, political, and cultural stage that collectively frames the context in which official action takes place, testing performance for an applied purpose, makes sense. Clearly, a public agency requires reliable input from a responsible source prior to making decisions about ways of delivering quality police services. Think of it this way, community policing establishes the police as professional experts on risk factors simply because the police often have experience with those factors or social facts (Ericson & Haggerty, 1997). If organized logically, information about their experiences is a valuable resource to others. At least, that's one way some residents view what the police know or what the police think they know. The police have an obligation in giving reliable information to constituents. Accepting the challenge, it should come as no surprise that some police agencies have produced significant findings for the public through explicit tests for the past two decades (Stephens, 1996). One example comes from a study, provided in part by police personnel, who tested the community policing initiatives in nine police agencies throughout the United States (Stevens, 2001a).[vii] What was recommended at the conclusion of that study was that:

> Herein is one advantage of sound research versus opinion and/or (police) experience. Reliable research contains methodological designs that can often produce dependable predictions while providing a body of knowledge that

enlightens policy-makers leading to informed decisions.... Guesses, although, often wrapped in experience, which of late, have been referred to as a form of profiling is what places many into harms way. It is important to note that while experience is a vital asset, once it is linked to sound research skills, the prospect for success is greater. Research can complement practical experience in many ways. However, research skills without experience can give rise to spuriousness, invalid findings, unreliable and in some cases unlawful recommendations. Research in the public sector, particularly justice agency research, is far different than research in the private sector recognizing litigation potentials and of more importance, issues of public trust.

Recalling many of the pains experienced by the agencies and their community members in this study, one issue is certain. If they had personnel with sound research skills, the path to success would have been more certain and they would have known where they were when they arrived there. In addition, they could have supported their position or achievements more accurately (much to the satisfaction of advocates and opponents). Therefore, the strongest recommendation flowing from those findings is police agencies should obtain the expertise of a trusted researcher in order to have alternative recommendations that might bring them closer to the values of a democratic society without compromising public safety (p.215).

The contributions of explicit procedures can help police executives do their job in an orderly and efficient manner bringing the agency closer to their mission. If their mission is centered in a community policing philosophy, then we could take some comfort in knowing that the people of the community are helping to govern their community, a process guaranteed through the Constitution.

Community Policing is a Partnership in Solving Community Problems Linked to Social Order

Make sense?

A practical goal of testing police performance is to ultimately forecast with some degree of certainty that something will happen—something will come from repairing street lights, or removing abandoned automobiles, or daily, helping kids with their homework. Something might be produced that will enhance the quality of live for community residents and for the police personnel who intersect with community members. In a word, predictability (remember our magic ball), and being able to see a little bit of the future can lead us to sound recommendations about the question or problem. Once we accept the changing nature of agencies and communities into consideration, there are five good reasons (and probably more you can think of) as to why an explicit test is more productive than other tests to understand the:

- ❖ **philosophy of community policing**
- ❖ **obstacles agencies are confronted with when they develop, implement, and maintain police services**
- ❖ **personal opinion**
- ❖ **funding**
- ❖ **public opinion**

Philosophy of Community Policing

Due to the philosophy of community policing and problem-solving commitments, explicit methods of evaluation is necessary to produce appropriate recommendations for change and to bring evidence to its reliability as a police strategy that can enhance quality of life levels for its constituents. Counting the number of arrests is not necessarily an appropriate method of ascertaining what changes are necessary or what is working in a police organization to accommodate a philosophy. The fact remains that community policing is not a program. It is not a series of meetings where command advises its audience about police accomplishments during that past month and new responses to criminal activity for the coming months. Furthermore, it is not a meeting under the thumb of the police, but control is in the hands of its elected officials that might include an officer here or there.

Community policing is an agency-wide way of doing business, different from the conventional hierarchy of command to a decentralized command. It is a different style of managerial skills that include the role of a facilitator instead of that of an enforcer because it is a partnership with the community members. It is a priority change from reacting to crime after it happens to that of reacting to crime before it happens or what can be called preventive service through community participation. It is not the prerogative of the police nor their Constitutional directive to control crime without community participation and responsibility. Officers and community members must be empowered (and trained) to resolve their own community problems in order to enhance public safety. This new relationship seeks mutual trust, respect, and responsibility. Therefore, cooperation demands some flexibility for the police and balancing of police priorities with the needs of the community. The role of the police in problem-solving is emphasized. Accordingly, measuring police performance is in the best interest of the community and the officers who serve a community (Carter & Radelet, 1999). It comes down to this for the police in the 21st century, should a department wish to provide community policing initiatives, they must become decentralized facilitators as opposed to a hierarchy of enforcers (Skogan, Hartnett, DuBois, Comey, Kaiser & Lovig, 1999; DuBois & Hartnett, 2001; Stevens, 2002a, 2002b, 1999a). Therefore, measuring the number of arrests might not be an efficient way to verify that community policing procedures are being maximized. As former Police Chief Dennis Nowicki of Charlotte, North Carolina (1998, p. 265) clarifies, "We no longer want to diffuse a problem, we want to solve it."

Obstacles

One answer might be that most police managers agree that there are always obstacles or what might be considered, opportunities originating inside and outside a police agency that must be dealt with when developing, implementing, and maintaining police policies and services especially in light of all the constant changes (Masterson & Stevens, 2002). Recalling that a community policing philosophy refers to among other things, empowerment to officers and community members to solve social problems linked to quality of life issues (which may or may not be crime related). Obstacles, therefore, occurring inside an agency can include a lack of empowerment to officers and to community members to make decisions that exist in the community. Certainty, the lack of authority to solve problems will lend itself to performance issues of the officer (and for the community). Then, too, should an officer be empowered to aid a community and rejects his or her responsibility, similar outcomes might be experienced by the community and the department. This empowerment issue cuts two ways—command can with hold sufficient authority to officers and community members and that authority when given, can be rejected (or taken advantage of). In either case, both obstacles are common among many departments.

If decision-making guidelines were broad within the community, then officer and community performance might be greater than expected. Therefore, empowering officers and community members to deal effectively with the problem solving process (decentralization of command) is a typical component of community policing policy. Results? As community problems are resolved through the initiatives of an officer, trust of the agency can grow among the residents, social order is enhanced, and some of the roots of crime (abandoned automobiles are removed, street lights are fixed, and gang members are playing sports) are addressed or neutralized (Stevens, 2002a).

Other internal obstacles might include the objections from an upper ranking officer who is required to change (cause) leadership styles from an authoritative commander to that of a facilitator (outcome) (Skogan, 1990). Testing the relationship between management style changes and management resistance might offer some valuable incites into this managerial style transformation, and at the same time reduce police officer stress (Stevens, 2000b, 1999d).

Obstacles outside an agency might include political intervention and suspect agendas held by community members and civic leaders. What is the best way to respond to obstacles? The results of standardized measures aid in making informed decisions about the future of police performance through recommendations that might suggest techniques about a community policing strategy or policy that can be changed to maximize outreach. Maybe, results could suggest techniques in the ways police intervention might enhance community participation, and/or how well community problem solving techniques impact fear of crime levels held by neighborhood residents.

These thoughts are consistent with Brodeur (1998) who argues that professional measurement procedures can tell police leaders when a police initiative or a community strategy is meeting their goals. These procedures can also help better understand police performance for purposes of accountability. That is, how well a department is progressing toward a collective goal and how well a specific officer is conducting the day-to-day business of providing police services. We also need to know how well a community is doing their job too since they are the other part of the partnership. Assessment of an agency or a community membership group is crucial for achieving accountability, for verifying how productive public and grant funds were spent, and for demonstrating outcomes of police strategies such as community policing initiatives (Oettmeier & Wycoff, 1997).

Personal Opinion

One of the rules often violated by most investigators relates to personal opinion or what can be called "subjective" as opposed to "objective" responses. There's good reason why this happens. Policy makers, police managers, and for that matter, you and me, view the world through our own experiences, values, and knowledge as the bases of judging the world.

> **Often times, it's not an event or a relationship that is significant but how that event or relationship is judged.**

Other times we might rely on stereotypes or our cultural understanding to help shape our thoughts when we're investigating a question. When an investigator is subjective (there is a tendency to prove his or her belief is right), a personal bias can alter the evidence producing suspect conclusions. This in turn might ultimately have an effect on public safety issues. For instance, whose idea will be used as a model of social order in a community? Should the police have a different viewpoint than the community, whose notion will be accepted and consequently determine police deployment practices. Police service calls might also be subject to a different set of priorities depending on whose view is considered as realistic.

Subjectivity produces an ethnocentric perspective. There are two deadly parts to this perspective: first—judging others, and other events on our own set of beliefs. And second, believing that our belief systems and/or judgments are right. In an earlier section, it was reported that it wasn't easy to measure the conduct of others since we tend to use our own experiences and/or culture in part as a way of judging the conduct of others. Now, it's becoming clear that this can be a bigger problem than one we're measuring. For instance, if a police officer believes that frightening a status offender (i.e. curfew violator, run away, and/or truant) with imprisonment will teach a juvenile a lesson, how often will the officer confine and/or deny due process rights to a status offender as opposed to assisting that offender with his or her homework? Sound strange? Maybe. But the point is well taken since some officers use different means to accomplish goals (most with good intention, of course).

Personal opinion or what can be called ethnocentric beliefs can easily bias an investigator's vision and as a result, alter the predictive value of a study because those unsuspecting investigators believe that they need to convince others of their ideals rather then allow evidence to speak for itself. Objective or professional behavior is difficult because many of us have difficulty leaving our cultural and personal baggage behind. Objectivity means that an investigator must remain nonjudgmental throughout the evaluation process.

 What groups of individuals can you think of that have a very specific idea about specific ideas of right and wrong? In what way can those beliefs produce conduct that may harm others?

Funding

Funding today is limited. Brodeur (1998) says that there is great competition for grant money among police agencies and city funds among varies municipal agencies. Quality measuring assessments can indicate where best to spend whatever resources are available. Then, too, there are many expectations about police strategies such as community policing. How well did the police meet those expectations? Is community policing—reality or rhetoric? For this reason, much of the motivation for conducting assessment is practical, economical, and professionally essential. It is a crucial tool for achieving accountability and for getting value for money in these times of budgetary constraint. Furthermore, community members want to know if one of their social agencies is doing the job within appropriate guidelines or not.

Public Opinion

Finally, how valid are our thoughts should we neglect to survey the very individuals we are trying to accommodate? Explicit tests of measurements bring to light what the public (or a targeted group under study) has to say about their life experiences. They have an opportunity to express their thoughts in a confidential way that might merit immediate attention. Ignoring their thoughts might be considered a travesty of justice and a little arrogant since the end result of police service is to enhance the quality of life experiences among constituents.

Causal Question and Rationale

Do cultural diverse community members engage in police decision-making processes? My idea is that the more community members, especially culturally diverse members, influence the decisions of the police, the greater the likelihood that public order will be enhanced. In effect, the community, especially the culturally diverse community, will become more active in policing themselves which includes becoming more responsible for crime and their own quality of life issues. The rationale is that the police can not and should not be responsible for crime control alone. One way this can be accomplished is through community policing initiatives which require decentralization of police command, empowerment of authority to police officers and community members within clearly defined limits, and a new managerial role to that of facilitator as found in Total Quality Management techniques.[viii] Police organizations are to emphasize preventative services to their constituents as opposed to reactive services.

Who Should Conduct a Test?

Eck and LaVigne (1994) implied earlier in this chapter that police personnel should conduct explicit methodological tests as opposed to outsiders such as consultants and volunteers. This is an interesting thought since government statistics reveal that most police officers may not necessarily have the skills to conduct a valid and reliable investigation, assuming advanced education and evaluative skills are related variables (Bureau of Justice Statistics, 1999). Would this be a similar thought as having correctional officers assessing prison related perspectives? One observation is that kindergarten teachers in public institutions have more requirements for employment than those individuals whom are generally hired to protect and control the lives of many people who should have far more expertise then teachers.

Nonetheless, it is true that police agencies across the country are involved in assessing police performance, and most utilize consultants and volunteers. For instance, Lincoln, Nebraska in partnership with a leading polling and consulting organization, developed a telephone survey to collect citizen perceptions of police services. The "Quality Service Audit" was developed as a way to validate a new, success-based talent selection system for police applicants and to provide community oriented police officers with relevant feedback about the quality of their contact with citizens (Citta, 1996).

Eventually, the Lincoln Police Department used new recruit officers to conduct the interviews by telephone. In this way those recruits became familiar with the department performance indicators and citizen expectations of service more efficiently than in riding along in a police cruiser. Each officer conducted approximately 100 interviews in an eighteen week period calling citizens who had received a citation, been involved in a traffic accident, and/or reported being the victim of a crime (Citta, 1996). Lincoln Police leaders used the feedback to identify and improve departmental systems and procedures that might have been barriers to delivering quality service and to determine training that helped elevate officer performance.

The media or the literature which ever term you prefer routinely reports a greater number of examples of explicit techniques conducted to provide police leaders with data about their partnership outcomes, but many departments utilized consultants and volunteers. For instance:

> Columbus Ohio Police Department developed and conducted an extensive survey of its citizens to determine how community policing should be implemented, what its objectives should be, and how it could be maintained. Because of those efforts, community participation was greater than expected when community policing was instituted in the city. Yet, at the same time, the anticipation of success was greatly expected by many individuals that lead to frustration and anger among many of policy makers, police command, officers, and community members. (Personal Communication with Commander, 2000).

> In an analysis of 15 Texas police agencies employing general survey methods, 10 agencies were administering mail surveys to measure attitudes of residents toward local police service, but only one had extended the scope of the survey to identify neighborhood problems (Surveys of Citizen Attitudes, 1996).

Surveys in the Reno, Nevada Police Department served as report cards from residents about police performance and image, extent of citizen fear, concerns about crime and quality of contact with department members. In the Peppermill Pop Project, for instance, residents, business owners, and property managers were asked to identify the number one crime problem; could it be solved or reduced; and, what they could do to improve the neighborhood (Kirkland & Glensor, 1992).

The St. Petersburg, Florida Police Department used a community-wide survey to identify citizen perceptions of neighborhood problems since 1991. Their survey instrument measured citizen perceptions on a variety of quality of life indicators and quality of police service (professional conduct, helpfulness, concern, etc.) Comparing 1994 survey results to 1991's baseline, St. Petersburg police leaders observed significant improvement in resident perceptions on these and other issues (Stephens, 1996).

Spokane, Washington Police Department, in collaboration with Washington State University, mailed a questionnaire to a random sample of city addresses to assess the public's attitudes toward police services from 1992 [521 respondents] to 1994 [1,134 respondents]. Results such as perceived improved service delivery; reduced fear of criminal victimization; and, increased citizen interest in working with the police were believed to be evidence of progress in the department's community policing efforts. The longitudinal survey also assisted police officers in identifying specific problems by individual neighborhoods and monitored trends over time (Thurman & McGarrell, 1995).

In March 1994, the Peel Region Police, using an independent marketing research firm, mailed survey questionnaires to over 10,000 randomly selected citizens. The survey, which included opinions and attitudes on community safety, police/citizen relationships and community-based policing, is the most extensive survey effort ever conducted by a Canadian municipal police agency (Peel Regional Police Survey, 1994).

Decatur, Alabama applied the concept of surveying the city's public housing tenants in evaluating the department's effectiveness in reducing crime. They asked questions on resident's fear of crime; impressions of police; opinion of how effective police were in controlling neighborhood crime; and what problems or concerns should receive priority status (Dutton, 1996).

The Madison Study

A study conducted by the Madison, Wisconsin Police Department changed the way management thought about conducting their own evaluations. After trial and error, the Madison Police Department (MPD) trained their own personnel to conduct performance evaluations (Masterson & Stevens, 2002).

Community policing has been a strategy practiced by the Madison, Wisconsin Police Department since the early 1980s. Measuring police performance, however, is a recent experience for them. Masterson and Stevens (2002) describe experiences of the MPD as the agency measured community policing performance in some of their challenged neighborhoods. One mission of the MPD was to better understand the needs of the residents in the neighborhoods through their own experiences. The MPD could have drawn professionals and volunteers from the University of Wisconsin at Madison.[ix] However, what makes their study unique is that measuring police performance in Madison, Wisconsin was conducted entirely by police personnel.[x] It is the hope of the MPD by reporting their experiences that other agencies will be encouraged to utilize a similar methodological design to measure performance in their communities, too as the advantages far outweigh the disadvantages.

Three lessons were learned from the Madison study. First, by listening to the individuals in the community, the MPD enhanced police decision-making practices that in turn, better served crime control issues through quality police services. Second, the MPD is only one of many participants that shape the meaning of quality police service. That is, it is the voice of their clients, through what they see, hear, and experience that should ultimately influence the levels of police service. Finally, MPD police personnel have greater opportunities to develop community policing initiatives and enhance some of their police skills when they conduct the research themselves.

Some of the community problems identified through neighborhood officer initiative included drug and alcohol abuse, low academic performance, lack of employment opportunities and job training, conflict, poor housing and disruptive tenants, inadequate recreational programs and undeveloped neighborhood leadership. Today, MPD's neighborhood officers are assisted by county social workers, state probation agents, and city building inspectors, all working from the same neighborhood offices. These decentralized networks have allowed the teams to focus on serious neighborhood problems that contribute to the outcomes of crime, dysfunctional families, and social disorder. Many of these notions find congruence with policing experts who argue that the police should not deal with crime alone and they should seek neighborhood participation within a problem-oriented approach (Goldstein, 1979; Kelling & Moore, 1988; Stevens, 1999b, 1999c).

In the early 1990s, Madison's high crime rate neighborhoods were suddenly deluged with the arrival of massage shipments of crack cocaine. As a means to contain the street level violence that became prevalent, the Neighborhood Intervention Task Force was created to supplement the efforts of patrol and neighborhood officers. The mission of the Task Force, referred to today as the Dane County Narcotics and Gang Task Force, was to interdict and prevent trafficking of street level drug sales. In the spring of 1992, the Task Force's efforts were enhanced when the United States Department of Justice recognized the City of Madison as one of 16 Weed and Seed sites. Subsequently, a grant was awarded to help fund and facilitate "weeding out" those responsible for the drugs and violence within the Weed and Seed designated neighborhoods so that "seeding" efforts could occur in hopes of making the neighborhoods once again self-sufficient. The community policing efforts of neighborhood officers was, in theory, to be the bridge between weeding and seeding.

A variety of measures were used to assess and evaluate MPD's Weed and Seed efforts. Hundreds of drug charges and convictions, thousands of dollars in recovered drugs and drug money, seizure of drug houses and assets, and the removal of numerous guns from neighborhood drug entrepreneurs, have been good conventional indicators of taskforce productivity. Yet, something was missing from the evaluation component. Do residents see the same improvements that the MPD sees? Do perceptions differ from one neighborhood to another? Where should future problem-solving strategies be directed? In order to assess resident perceptions, non-conventional evaluation mechanisms were developed including the use of neighborhood officers and police recruits as interviewers. Of course, those officers were trained not by cops but by professional researchers. Consultants and volunteers would have to wait until social order returned to those neighborhoods. True, some members of the community might have been intimated by police officers asking questions, and there is little response to that thought, nonetheless the results speak for themselves.

The MPD felt that if their challenged neighborhoods became safer and better organized that their residents were more likely to be more outspoken, better educated about issues affecting their lifestyles, and more willing to discuss problems within their community. Also, with their participation also came the opportunity for the department to assume the facilitative role of management at the community meetings and at solving problems since those community members were better prepared to deal with community problems (Skogan, 1998; Stevens, 1999d). There is the thought that if those early studies in the late 1980s were police officers in the field, they could have been able to predict the advent of the huge cocaine problem that engulfed the high-risk neighborhoods in Madison. That is, officers are trained to anticipate problems, and they have a legal responsibility to address anticipations of unlawful conduct—consultants and volunteers are not seen by residents as having neither the responsibility or the authority to make things change for the better (Stevens, 2000b).

Madison and Social Order

Overall, the MPD believes that social order can be accomplished when community members participate in police decisions. Gaining neighborhood input is best left to police officers since there is much to gain for everyone involved. Compelling evidence has been presented that demonstrates the typical community member would be more honest with an officer than others and that some members of the community who lie about many things would lie or misrepresent to anybody even a student interviewer. Strong neighborhood associations, their visible and trusted leadership, an active community center, and the active presence of police officers all contribute to a well-informed and involved community that is more likely to identify problems, report them to authorities, and work with the department to solve those problems. Then, too, officers who are less experienced than others now have an opportunity to learn to rely on some of the information provided by the community and the bridge narrows between the "them and us" or phased another way, that thin blue line gets smaller rather than bluer (Stevens, 2000b, 1999c). Who should conduct police evaluations—police officers, especially after being trained as evaluators.

With that said, the question arises as to how police agencies should gather data to aid them in making decisions about police services that might include deployment, tactical limits, and hiring and disciplinary guidelines among officers. How should information be gathered about other issues such as levels of social order and social problems from the perspective of the individuals whom the agency serves?

End of Part II Section

Part III: The Stages of Testing Police Practice

Part III is a practical guide to aid investigators as they develop and conduct their own test.[xi] There are variations offered by other investigators that might appear to be more credible and in keeping with traditional research methodology, but we no longer live in the confined, rigid highbrow world of the twentieth century. However, since every test and organizational goal are different as is the expertise of every investigator, reviewing those traditional perspectives and adding them to your knowledge base along with the following discussion will help you get a better sense of the task at hand. Therefore, accept this guide as a working draft to advance your skill level as an investigator. Also, be mindful that the following has been utilized in a variety of settings to help develop the explicit investigator skill of university students and public agency personnel such as sworn officers (from chiefs to recruits) to human service workers (from directors to interns) and private organizations from corporate managers (from CEOs to an apprentice) and to corporate trainers and mental health personnel of all varieties with some success.

Here's how it's done

Once they developed a suitable question leading to a cause and an expectation (which should be answered in the conclusion of a study), they're ready. But, it goes without saying that professional writing skills as those practiced by the American Psychological Association should be adhered too (more about this later in the section). Additionally, writers must understand that they are not writing for themselves. They are writing for organizations, institutions, and policy makers. They are writing for their readers. Therefore, an efficient investigator addresses issues that influence those readers. Thus, objectivity is key. Testing performance in an explicit format consists of all the activities that pertain to five stages: Media Review and Problem Formulation; Test Design and Sample; Gather and Process Information; Results; and an Analysis of Results. Naturally, at the end of the road, an evaluator disseminates the information to ultimately change behavior. Therein lays the mission of evaluation—to change behavior.

Stage One: Develop the Question to Examine Media Search and Problem Formulation

State the question you will investigate followed by the causal relationship which should include both your causal factors and its expected outcome. Here is the question and causal relationship I'm investigating: Do culturally diverse community members engage in police decision-making processes? The belief is that the more community members, especially culturally diverse members, influence the decisions of the police, the greater the likelihood that public order will be enhanced. Public order is defined as crime control, reduction of the fear of crime, and an enhancement of quality of life experiences among community constituents.

It is expected that in Stage One the problem under investigation will be framed in a coherent and documented (cite your references) narrative. For me, that means that the causal factor or variable (community members influencing police decisions) and the outcome (public order) are identified, defined, and discussed from various viewpoints including those viewpoints that disagree with my perspective. An important anticipated question that I must answer in my own narrative follows: why should the community influence police decisions? In my study, I need to articulate under what conditions community influences are a good idea and under what conditions it might be a bad idea. To be an efficient investigator, try to anticipate obvious questions that readers might raise and address those questions in the narrative before they ask them. That is, a critical discussion needs to be presented about influences that effect your causal explanation such as historical accounts, public policy, and maybe even current attitudes from the perspectives of the public, the police, and the policy makers.

An investigator should address various ways in which the causal component (community influence) can alter the value (as to degrees) of the outcome expected (public order). Stage One includes a review of other experiences to aid a reader to better understand the problem—what have other police agencies, consultants, and organizations reported about bringing an agency toward a community policing philosophy?[xii] Your job is to search the media. This search can be conducted at websites, libraries (usually academic libraries are best), and/or justice academy archives. For example, my search produced 38 references (all which must be cited in the narrative and correspond with the reference page). Much of what I learned about police agency policy can be found on the web. Generally, a good investigation requires a minimum of 14 references of which one-half should generally represent investigations from the professional press[xiii] and one-half should represent opinion pieces from the popular media.[xiv]

Following is a list of good search engines that might help find information:

- Yahoo www.yahoo.com
- Web Crawler www.webcrawler.com

- Alta Vista www.altavista.com
- HotBot www.hotbot.com
- Lycos www.lycos.com
- Excite www.excite.com
- InfoSeek www.infoseek.com

In your narrative answer the question: why is your study important? Are there ethical issues that need to be addressed? I suppose one way to explain what you're doing in this stage is to suggest that your task is to allow your reader to get a clear picture of the things you are going to investigate. Caution: students like to find information that supports their ideas, but it is in your best interest to gather information that doesn't support your point of view too in order to help your reader get a good look at the question being investigated. Also, a writer must remain objective throughout this process. Objectivity suggests that a writer avoids making a judgment one way or another about any of the information gathered. It's best to stay away from words in your narrative that lend themselves to a judgment call such as: surprisingly, shockingly, and unexpectedly.

On a separate sheet of paper, write your references as a result of your media search. Write a brief statement on how each reference is linked to your question. Now, prepare a narrative using all your references. (Note: In the last process, do not push all your sentences together).

Stage Two: Design Your Test and Identify Your Sample

Knowledge is inevitably built on experience and observation. Hence, the crux of a valid applied test is centered on getting information or data.

Data collection techniques or test design occurs through a variety of ways (i.e. observation, experiment, content analysis, and direct inquiry—interviews, surveys, and sample identification; see Table 2). The design explains how you will perform your direct or indirect observations to obtain data and how you will process it. Table 2 might help you select a design or group of designs suitable for your particular test. Whatever design is used, a narrative must be offered about your design; why it was selected and how it was processed.

Observation

Observation is a design used by many investigators because it is relatively easy to accomplish. While attending community policing meetings, I was able to observe the "give and take" between police officers and community members. For some tests, observation might be the best method available. As one can imagine, cultural anthropologists might use this technique to study rural civilizations, and sociologists might use it to study motorcycle gangs. Observation means just that—to observe people in action. Sometimes, investigators might go further. That is, they might participate in the group. Sometimes when sociologists investigate gang members they might join the gang and report on the gang's activities. Of course, there are many problems but advantages, too from participant observers. In what way could participant observers be at an advantage and in what way might they be at a disadvantage? Observations produce first hand experience with real-life activities, but apply to only the case being observed. And results are only as professionally drawn as is the observer.

Two more points, sometimes observer biases occurs. That is, observers follow an initial tendency to rate certain objects or subjects in a biased manner. When this phenomena occurs it is called the Halo Effect. Also, when subjects know they are being studied, their conduct changes. This is called the Hawthorne Effect. Both are common effects that might change the conduct.

Experiment

An experiment is manipulating variables to ascertain their outcome on the sample in the field or in the laboratory. Ease of testing theories and ease of controlling conditions of the experiment. One concern is that an investigator's presence will certainly influence outcomes in the field. In the laboratory, individuals might act differently than when outside. This method is used often by psychologists and biologists. It probably isn't as efficient when studying community policing or other models for a variety of reasons. Can you identify some problems that may surface when testing police performance using an experiment?

Content Analysis

Content Analysis is another method of testing performance. In this design, primarily only other studies would be used to make decisions about the causal question. Sometimes, converting statistical explanations to verbal explanations from other studies would exclusively be used. Content Analysis is best when used to investigate historical information. One point that needs to be made is that interpretation of other studies would more likely be subjective than objective explanations.

Direct Inquiry: Interviews, Surveys, and Samples

Lastly, interviews and surveys are what can be referred to as direct inquire designs. Usually, these designs include large samples that have input through surveys and/or from interviews. Often, the two techniques are merged. The Madison police, for example, used surveys and officers took it into the field to complete with community members (Appendix I), and when they finished the survey, they asked the respondent other questions about their perception of public safety issues in the community. Although this is not a recommended method to follow, doing something rather than nothing brings us closer to our goals. One word to the wise, however, is that often when human subjects are included in a study, getting their consent might be advisable, and in many cases may be required by certain institutions. One way of protecting the identity of participants, organizations, or communities is the use of pseudonyms (false names) in publications.

Interviews: Once the officer from the Madison Police Department finished completing the survey, other issues were discussed and those verbal results (qualitative explanations) were compared with the data (quantitative explanations) from the surveys. However, that is not to say that the same is best in reverse. An interview should not consist of asking individuals questions from the survey. Another method might be to interview one sample, and survey a different but similar set of individuals to see how closely their responses are related. Differences and/or similarities between survey results and interview results should be explained.

Interviews produce rich responses. Phone interviews can be conducted easily and inexpensive. But face to face inquiry can produce excellent information. One approach to interviewing is to develop a short list of general topic questions for the respondents such as: "tell me about your job?" As the respondent reveals information, since the interviewer is trying to build rapport (trust) with the respondent, an interviewer should:

❖ listen attentively

❖ refrain from judgmental comments, and

❖ use nonverbal cues to ask the respondent to continue

That is, When interviewers are talking, they tend to learn less than when they are listening. The mission of the interviewer is to gain as much information as possible from the participant, not the other way around. As a respondent gives general information, specific questions should be asked by the interviewer in order to gain concrete examples of those experiences. "Can you give me an idea as to how that works," an experienced investigator might ask a participant even when the interviewer has an expertise in the subject mentioned.

However, if a respondent takes issue with an investigator during both the survey or the interview, what those participants tend to report might be different among different investigators. For instance, if an Irish American, older male were interviewing or distributing a survey to African American females, those participants might respond one way as compared to an African American female researcher of similar age as the sample. In general, interviews are time consuming and can be costly, but seemingly a wealth of information can be produced through this method.

Surveys: In my study on community members, I developed a survey to be used at community meetings (See Appendix II) and graduate students who often were from the countries represented by the sample, distributed those surveys along with many other students.

Developing the survey itself is a difficult process and often requires a great deal of time along with a lot of input (from many sources), and patience. Even when it is completed to your satisfaction, it should be tested and revised to get the bugs out. In Appendix I of this chapter are surveys used by the Madison, Wisconsin Police Department, and in Appendix II there is a survey developed for this chapter. It was used in the following jurisdictions: Alexandria, Virginia; Boston, Massachusetts; Columbia, South Carolina; Columbus, Ohio; Miami, Florida; Midland, Texas; Palm Beach County, Florida; and Sacramento, California.

Surveys generally consist of several components:

❖ **Confidentiality statement: use of survey**

❖ **Qualifier Question: (e.g. what district of Madison do you life in?)**

❖ **Demographics: (e.g. length of time in the community; age, renter/owner, gender, ethnic identity/race)**

❖ **Questions relating to your causal question (never use your causal question in surveys, for instance, if studying corruption or alcoholic abuse among narcotic officers— don't brother with questions that ask: are you corrupt or an alcoholic? In those surveys, the outcome should never be in the survey question—answers might be okay).**

Students are encouraged to develop a survey consisting of 25 questions since those questions generally will fit on two pages (brevity aids survey performance and survey management). Of 25 questions, 18 should relate to causal issues, 2 should relate to outcome issues, and 5 to demographic issues (age, gender, job and so forth). One of the demographic questions should be a "qualifier." If you're measuring community performance, ask participants where they live. Surveys should have ample space between each question with ample margins (but not margined justified) around the page. It goes without saying that the survey shouldn't contain spelling errors or words that your sample might not understand or appreciate. KISS here: that is, Keep it Simple and Short! Don't ask questions to fill space. Each question must have a purpose and surveys with a large number of questions such as 50 or more are probably too long.

The wording of questions and answers (if closed-ended) must relate to the people being surveyed. That is, the words selected must be in the vocabulary of the respondents. Each question should probably contain a set of answers (give answers that make sense) that a respondent can check or circle. The surveys in Appendix I and II contain answers for the convenience of the respondents. Surveys with closed-ended answers are faster to complete, easier to record and to tabulate. Give "way out" answers. That is, if a respondent doesn't want to answer a particular question, there is a way out for them, such as a "don't know," or "not sure," or "other" type responses. That includes answers that are "Yes" or "No" (should include a "don't know" response).

How do you develop questions and answers? For best results, try not to use your outcome expectation in any question. For instance, when examining my idea that the more community members influence police decisions, the more public order would be enhanced, therefore, any part of public order can not be used in the questions, but it can be used in a closed-ended response. In order to further validity (accuracy),[xv] participants must report to the investigator the answer as opposed to the other way around.[xvi] By putting your outcome in a question, a participant could easily guess what's on your mind and might try to win your approval or the approval of their friends as they conduct the survey by offering an inaccurate response. For instance:

1. In the past year, has your neighborhood become: (Check One Only)

A much safer place to live	_____
A safe place to live	_____
About the same	_____
An unsafe place to live	_____
A very unsafe place	_____

Of course, there are a variety of other reasons why a participant might respond inappropriately including incriminating themselves in unacceptable or illegal activity. Be mindful that when developing interview questions of questions for your survey that many of us have been programmed to respond to certain questions with specific "socially approved responses" or socially approved rhetoric. For instance, if you ask an offender if he committed the crime of child molestation, most often what answer might he give? How often would you guess that he would say that he was molested when a child? Ask a cop if she ever arrested anyone based primarily on gender or race, what answer could you expect?

There are many ways to discover truth and some of those ways have to do with finding social indicators. A social indicator might include asking criminals about their early life experiences. Ask police officers about their arrest experiences and ask community police supervisors about their notions about crime and justice. Are you getting the idea? When quizzing alcoholics ask about punctuality and work experiences. You're looking for indicators and patterns. Therefore, from the media search you conducted, you would learn or confirm information you know already about certain indicators suggestive of certain behavioral patterns or conditions about others. When I investigated corruption among narcotic officers, obviously I couldn't ask if a respondent were corrupt or not. I had to uncover social indicators of what corrupt behavior looks like and ask the officers about those indicators.[xvii] How ever you develop your survey, discuss the primary points of its process so that your readers have an idea about that process. For instance, the survey used in my study as shown in Appendix II was developed over a period of time by the principle researcher in collaboration with police practitioners. In reviewing surveys they used at their departments, certain ideas came to mind. For instance, the Madison Wisconsin survey had some relevant questions that, in part, were developed for my survey. Also in reading the Bureau of Justice Assistance's (1992*) Helping Communities Mobilize against Crime, Drugs, and Other Problems*, the researcher learned much about what makes communities work. Lastly, Skogan's et al (1999) compelling work in Chicago helped the writer frame questions, too. The finished product was reviewed by many colleagues including Jill DuBois in Chicago, Captain Michael Masterson in Madison, and Professor Kurt Kerley at the University of Tennessee in

Knoxville. The survey was tested on several groups prior to being distributed nationally. Adjustments were made accordingly. (It is expected that a narrative similar to what you have read above is in your method's section or Stage Two of your work).

Some of the disadvantages of surveys are that the questions developed can not easily be changed once the study is underway because it's hard to go back and ask respondents to retake a survey. Results from surveys are reduced to statistical explanations including averages (i.e. average age of your respondents).

Your design for your investigation could be seen as one of the following:

Table 2   Investigation Designs

Method	Characteristics	Advantages	Disadvantages
Observation	Watching individuals at community meetings. Participating in community meetings and/or concealing oneself watching gang activity from a van.	First hand experiences with real-life activities.	Observations might apply to only the case being observed. And results are only as professionally drawn as the observer.
Experiment	Manipulating variables to ascertain their outcome on the sample in the field or in the laboratory.	Ease of testing theories and ease of controlling conditions of the experiment.	Investigator's presence will influence outcomes in the field. In the laboratory, individuals might act differently than when outside.

Content Analysis	Evaluating other studies. Or converting statistical explanations to verbal explanations.	Time. Also, may be best way to evaluate historical information.	The interpretation of other studies would more likely be subjective than objective explanations.
Direct Inquiry	Surveys. Interviews.	Large samples can have input through questionnaires. Interviews produce richer responses. Phone interviews can be conducted easily and inexpensive.	Questions developed can't be changed once study is underway easily. Results from surveys are reduced to statistical explanations. Interviews are time consuming, can be costly, but allow more flexibility. Phone interviews lack face to face advantages.

Sample

In sum, Stage Two consists of articulating the design you will use to test your idea. But it also includes a plan for sample selection, collection, recording results, and statistical (averages, percents, cross tabulations, chi square, other) methods to be used. A population to be studied must be selected (for me that meant residents in several cities across the U.S. including Boston). The total survey participants numbered 2,010 in my study.

A sample of at least twenty-five participants can produce results that can provide a window of information. It goes without saying that the individuals in the sample should not be family or personal friends of the investigator. Of course, the number of participants can go as high as several thousand individuals depending on the resources of the investigator/s and the size of the population of the group in question. Whichever sample is selected, a narrative is expected that reports the decisions made by the investigator.

All of the participants of a test should have something in common, and should be relevant to the causal question. My sample, for example, were all residents in cities where community policing programs were underway and most of the respondents reported that they participated in community policing meetings. How you select your sample is relevant too and it goes to the credibility of the findings. That is, if you were studying crime, ask criminals; if you were investigating schools, ask students; if you were examining arrest rates, ask the police. That is, always go to the source when possible. So, if you were examining water, ask fish. An efficient investigator knows that almost every member of a targeted population must have an equal chance of being in the study.

In my study, my assistants and I attended community policing meetings and had permission from the leaders of those organizations to distribute a survey to the members present. There was only one version of the survey used in all cases (more about survey development in the next section). The survey had been translated from English into Chinese, Portuguese, and Spanish (and translated back into English when evaluating the results). Once participants completed the survey, it was collected, surveys were brought to my office, each survey was numbered, and graduate students and/or myself depending on who was available recorded answers to each question in a computer grid.

Which members of the community did not have an equal change of completing my survey? Those who didn't come to the meetings, of course. Maybe they were on vacation, or ill, or seating in a classroom. How many people in a community might not join a community meeting? Why? What about their ideas on police performance? One of the tasks of a good investigator is to try to get as many members in a targeted population to be heard. Put another way, in what way can an unscrupulous and/or an ignorant investigator bias results?

Some police agencies have a survey online. If a survey is only available online, residents without a computer might not be able to respond to questions. If Walmart is the only place in a city where an investigator asks shoppers about policing, what members of the community are not likely to be represented? If the survey is conducted in the evening, shoppers who work at night won't be represented. If the survey is conducted at the local community college, depending on the time and the building (biology— natural sciences, or behavioral science, or athletic building) can the survey results be biased? Officers in Madison, Wisconsin who walked their "beat" and knocked on doors asked questions of residents they encountered, which individuals were probably underrepresented in their test (see Appendix II)?

Good investigators allow for as many of the intended population to be heard. But you can't get them all or even close to it. Also, examining an inappropriate sample could also alter results. Can you imagine groups of individuals that might alter an investigator's findings one way or another?

Finally, much of the time, permission needs to be obtained from the appropriate individuals to conduct a survey at Walmart (the manager) or at the community college (the president), or where ever the survey is conducted. An investigator establishes in advance access to a survey population. It isn't automatic that specific populations (prisoners, patents, councilors, community members) are available because you're a surveyor or a cop. Allow time to get approval and its best to get it in writing for your files so that there are no misunderstandings. In the agreement letter, indicate among other things who will conduct the survey, which days/nights, and at what times. Identify your sample and explain how you'll gain access to your sample.

Stage Three: Gather and Process Information

Gather and process data using guidelines explained in Stage Two. Data are assembled, classified, and organized in a way that helps investigators test their question. This might include codes for each question and each answer on a survey, data spread sheets to help organize and interpret the data, and/or transcribing interviews that were conducted by using recorders or notes written by an investigator. Depending on the size of the sample and the instruments used to develop the data, might depend on supporting components to help in this stage. For example, large scale surveys might be best left to computerized statistical packages that can help validate or compute data using a number of statistical tests such as chi square, or t-tests. However, it is recommended not to learn statistical formulas, if you are not comfortable with statistics. Let computer programs assist you in this end of it, since that is why they were designed in the first place. Get some experience with a statistical program. How ever you develop this stage, a narrative is expected and should be part of the narrative developed in Stage Two. Some researchers call Stage Two and this section the methodology or method section of testing your hunch.

Stage Four: Results

Describe the results produced from the test design in a clear and logical manner (that means without your opinion). How often do some of your findings parallel some of the experiences of the media discussions which are in your narrative in Stage One? Say so. That is, write something like "this finding is consistent with what the Madison Police Department found when they surveyed residents in their community." Be sure to cite it appropriately.

Accuracy and significance of findings are assessed in terms of their validity and reliability. Validity refers to the degree to which a study or the social instrument such as a questionnaire actually measured what it was intended to measure.[xviii] Reliability refers to the degree to which a study or social instrument provides consistently accurate results. If the study were conducted by another police agency using similar methods and designs they should be able to produce similar results or another words, the findings can be repeated or replicated. Some investigators believe that tests that can not be replicated are suspect. Why do you think they suggest that? How ever you develop this stage, a narrative is expected and a Table highlighting your findings would be helpful. Often this investigator suggests that a Table should be developed first to help you stay organized.

Stage Five: Analysis of the Results (Conclusion)

With all the data available, what are your thoughts or your conclusions? Answer the question you originally asked: Do culturally diverse community members engage in police decision-making processes? In my conclusion, it is that question that will take center stage. In what way has the causal question been supported? Link major points of the conclusion to the media (experiences of others as reported in Stage One). Make the leap from specifics to generalizations (inductive reasoning). What are your recommendations based on the findings? Link sample to population or larger population if feasible. How ever you develop this stage, a narrative is expected. Finally, develop a brief summary or Abstract of your entire study in 150 words or less.

Format

Of vital importance is the professional writing format of your study, depending on your audience. One strong recommendation is that the

American Psychological Association (APA) citation style be followed throughout your work. An inexpensive manual can be purchased online.[xix] The following recommendations should be considered when writing your study:

- ❖ paper size and color: 8 ½ X 11 and white paper with black ink
- ❖ font selections and point size: New Times Roman & 12
- ❖ margins: 1 inch around the page
- ❖ double-spaced, except single spaced with indented quotes
- ❖ justified margins throughout work, except tables, references (only on reference page), survey
- ❖ appropriate citations
- ❖ citations must match references in regard to spelling and publication dates
- ❖ reference page
- ❖ references should match the citations and vise versa and should match the source of those references
- ❖ endnotes at end of chapter
- ❖ spelling and grammar should be as accurate as possible
- ❖ 3rd person is more appropriate than 1st person
- ❖ tense agreement is required
- ❖ stay away from quotes—interpret what others say and cite accordingly
- ❖ Above all, be consistent

Two last points. Once you have completed a final draft, develop a short executive summary or what is referred to as an Abstract. That is, in one sentence or so, tell your reader about each Stage of development. Be sure to mention your sample, and how closely the findings came to meeting your idea. Make a recommendation based on your findings, too. Generally, an abstract should not exceed 150 words.

Finally, it is strongly advised that you have someone look over your work to be sure things look right. For instance, this work was reviewed by Professors Nina Silverstein, CPCS and Xiaogang Deng, Department of Sociology, and Melissa Driscol, University of Massachusetts Boston. As one example, check over this work including its citations, references, margins, font, point, and so on…Following this format gives your work a professional appearance and after all, you have spent a lot of time with a study and I'm sure that you'd want it to appear as professional as possible. One question that can be raised about following a professional style of writing is that generally:

If people don't believe the message because of numerous mistakes, will they believe the messenger?

We all have a lot to say, and style is a big part of the saying. When things aren't right with style, then we could expect others to wonder about our abilities. Does that make sense?

In Sum

In sum there are five parts to your investigation:

- Stage One: What question you are going to investigate?
  - Explain it
  - Media Search
  - Problem Formulation
  - Anticipate Questions of Readers
  - Relevance of Investigation

- Stage Two: How will you test your question and who is your sample?
  - Sample
  - Design

- Stage Three: Gather and Process Data.
  - Collect it
  - Code it
  - Spread Sheet
  - Statistics

- Stage Four: What were the results produced from your design?
  - Link some of your findings to your references

- Stage Five: What do you really think about what you found?
  - Your opinion is valid here based on the evidence
  - Answer the investigated question
  - Link your opinion to some of your references

Tables, Endnotes, Copy of Survey, and References at end of work

MAKING SENSE

After reading this work, you might get the impression that measuring performance is laborious and its results or recommendations often border on the obvious. You might even say that measuring police intervention and activity produces what is already known or what can be referred to as sensible or common sense.

> **Yet, if common sense is one of the best ways to understand the world, why do some organizations make so many mistakes or take longer to meet organizational goals?**

Making decisions especially informed decisions, makes sense. Yet, it involves using the human senses of sight and hearing to observe the social world. The 21st century police officer can not make decisions centered in commonsense notions in a dynamic and pluralistic society. As Trojanowicz and Dixon (1974) argue, such notions "facilitate uncritical observations which lead to erroneous assumptions and decisions. They are the basis of prejudices and often biased judgements that obscure truth" (p. 153). Observations can be checked for accuracy by other investigators using a similar design. Therefore, a good test is very public and an open path to knowledge. Because a question can be replicated or tested by others, the pitfalls of bias, emotion, and distorted reasoning might be reduced.

The process of establishing a test on performance and drawing conclusions from observations must follow the rules of logic. But no scientific truth is ever accepted on the bases of logic alone. That is, even common sense ideals might not be as true as we think. For instance, we might  expect that behavior under the same police leadership and command, produces similar community policing outcomes. Specifically, in Chicago, beat team sergeants answering to the same lieutenant seemed to have a greater impact on community policing performance in their patrol areas than their supervisor (Skogan, et al, 1999).

What's more, a reality that should be understood by every community policing planner is that every police agency has its own unique features, due in part to its history, location, tax base, officer demographics, prior experiences and memories of agency and community members, police management and policy makers, and intervention experiences by other private and public institutions in the jurisdiction. Therefore, it is unlikely that any single police agency or model of policing strategy such as community policing, no matter how eloquent the model, can be promoted as "best" or normal. So common sense is good, but in considering community outcomes, there are many variables that effect outcomes that we neglected.

Finally, there are many similarities between police investigators and behavioral investigators or researchers. Both the officer and the behaviorist attempt discovery through a systematic, objective process where the tools used to gather evidence are guarded for validity. Also, both investigators largely utilize deductive reasoning where typical assumptions are made and conclusions are drawn that appear to be logically connected with those assumptions. For example, "All men are mortal. Aristotle is a man. Therefore, Aristotle is moral." During an investigation, any event that needs to be explained provides a foundation for deductive thinking or rationale building. Through data gathering and analysis, investigators learn whether their deductions are valid. If the data suggest those deductions should be questioned, further testing or gathering of evidence is necessary. These ideas are consistent with researchers in general who advance the idea that even if the results support certain deductions, further testing is ordinarily conducted, since investigators want to be certain of their conclusions in order to accomplish their mission.

In Summary

Ultimately, the goal of a professional investigator is the construction of an idea or a model that describes a way to better understand the development of strategies intended to address the issues of quality service regardless what that service provides. Finally, should you wish to review the final data from the test described in this work, contact the writer at dennis.stevens@umb.edu.

EXERCISES

Exercise 1: According to the author, why conduct a test of police officers, doctors, human service personnel, councilors, students, and/or professors job performance?

_____

_____

_____

_____

Exercise 2: Why would anyone want to know outcomes of rehabilitation procedures, intervention, advertising campaigns, retail sales, or incarceration?

_____

_____

_____

_____

Exercise 3: Below are "fixed" methods of evaluating police activities. In what way can these activities aid the police to better deliver their services?
- arrests _____
- patrol stops & citations _____
- calls for service _____
- response time _____
- complaints against officers _____
- dollar amounts _____

Exercise 4: In thinking about Exercise 3, what about where you work or where you want to work? In what way do they evaluate their programs, policies, or strategies?

_____

_____

_____

_____

Exercise 5: When you're thinking about a program, policy, or strategy, how would you evaluate them in order to make a good recommendation—a recommendation that a future promotion for you, might depend on?

_____

_____

_____

_____

Exercise 6: Identify a good idea that you want to understand better.

_____

_____

_____

_____

Exercise 7: Break down your idea. Identify:

Cause: _____

Outcome: _____

If this, then that (predictive value): _____

Why do you want to investigate it? _____

_____

Exercise 8: Identify and explain a social fact?

_____
_____
_____
_____

Exercise 9: How many common sense explanations can you think of that might not be realistic when examined? Identify one that applies to education, one that applies to work, and one that applies to the concept of success.

Education: _____
Work: _____
Success: _____

Exercise 10: Under what conditions would it be right to "mask" or hide certain (public or police) conduct?

_____
_____
_____
_____

Exercise 11: What about your "ideal" job. Under what conditions would it be okay to hide certain official or unofficial behavior? (Identify your ideal job, first)

_____
_____
_____
_____

Exercise 12: Can you come up with a few reasons why an applied test as compared to a pure test might be more useful to another type of business other than policing?

_____

_____

_____

_____

Exercise 14: Identify specific groups that hold suspect perspectives about other groups.

_____

_____

_____

_____

Exercise 15: Describe the outcomes produced through ethnocentric perspectives of the groups you mentioned in Exercise 14.

_____

_____

_____

_____

Exercise 16: The following list of references has several errors: Your job is to find those errors and bring these references up to APA standards. Are all of these references cited in the body of this chapter? Concerning your own work, are all of your resources on the reference page cited within the context of your work? (Authors' names are spelled correctly). Circle errors.

REFERENCES

American Psychological Association. (1994). Publication manual for the American Psychological Association, 4th edition. (On-Line), Available: http://www.apa.org/books/4200040.html

Berger, P.L. (1963). *Invitation to sociology: A humanistic perspective.* Garden City, NJ: Anchor Books.

Bittner, E. (1974). A theory of the police. In H. Jacob (Ed.), *Potential for reform of criminal justice.* (p. 17-44). Beverly Hills: Sage.

Brodeur, J.P. (1998). *How to recognize good policing: Problems and issues.* Thousand Oaks, CA: Sage.

Bureau of Justice Statistics. (2000). Sourcebook of Criminal. [On-line], Available:

Carter, D.L., & Radelett, L.A. (1999). *The police and the community.* 6th edition. Upper Saddle River, NJ: Prentice Hall.

DeLeon-Granados, W. (1999). *Travels through crime and place.* Boston: Northeastern Press.

DuBois, J., & Hartnett, S.M. (2002). Making the community side of community policing work: What needs to be done. In Dennis J. Stevens (Ed.) *Policing and Community Policing.* Upper Saddle River, NJ: Prentice Hall.

Durkheim E. (1933; 1984). The division of labor in society: Translated by W.D. Hall. NY: The Free Press.

Erickson, R.V., & Haggerty, K.D. (1997). *Policing the risk society*. Toronto: University of Toronto Press.

Goldstein, H. (1977). *Policing a free society*. Cambridge, MA: Ballinger.

Goldstein, H. (1990). *Problem-oriented policing*. NY: McGraw Hill.

Kelling, G.L., & Moore, M.H. (1999). The evolving strategy of policing. In Victor E. Kappeler (Ed.), *The police and society*, (p. 2-26). Prospect Heights, IL: Waveland Press.

Kirkland, R., & Glensor, R. (1992). Community oriented Policing and Problem Solving Fepartment report. Reno, NE: Reno Police Department.

Klockers, C.B. (1988). The rhetoric of community policing. In J.R. Greene & S.D. Mastrofski (Eds.), *Community policing: Rhetoric or Reality* (pp.239-258). NY: Preger.

Kruttschnitt, C., Ward, D., & Sheble, M.A. (1987). Abuse-resistant youth: Some factors that may inhibit violent criminal behavior. Social Focus, 66(2), 501-519.

Manning, P. K. (1997). *Police work: The social organization of policing*. Prospect Heights, IL: Waveland Press.

McElroy, J.E., Cosgrove, C.A., & Sadd, S. (1993). *Community policing: The CPOP in New York*. Newbury Park, CA: Sage Publishing.

Masterson, M., & Stevens, D.J. (2002). The value of measuring community policing performance in Madison Wisconsin. In Dennis J. Stevens (Ed.) Policing and Community Partnerships (Pages 77-93). Upper Saddle River, NJ: Prentice Hall.

Milofsky, A. (2000, January/February). Examining police behavior under Nazi rule offers contemporary lessons on moral responsibility and civil liabilities. *Community Policing Exchange. VII*(30), 3.

Nowicki, D.E. (1998). Mixed messages. In Geoffrey Alpert and Alex Piquero (EDS.) *Community Policing*, (p. 265-274), Prospect Heights, IL: Waveland Press.

Oettmeier, T.N., & Wycoff, M.A. (1997). Personnel performance evaluations in the community policing context. In Geoffrey Alpert and Alex Piquero (Eds.) *Community Policing*, (p. 275-306), Prospect Heights, IL: Waveland Press.

Peel Regional Police Survey of Attitudes and Opinions. (1994, March). Benchmark Study. Brampton, Ontario.

Popenoe, D. (2000). *Sociology.* Upper Saddle River, NJ: Prentice Hall.

Police Executive Research Forum. (1996). *Themes and variations in community policing.* Washington DC: Police Executive Research Forum.

Reno, J., Dwyer, J.C., Robinson, L., & Gist, N.E. (1997, September). Crime Prevention and Community Policing: A Vital Partnership. Washington DC: Bureau of Justice Assistance Justice Assistance: Crime Prevention and Community Policing: A Vital Partnership. NCJ 166819. [Online], Available: *http://www.ojp.usdoj.gov/BJA*

Reiner, R. (1998). Process or product? Problems of assessing individual police performance. In Jean-Paul Brodeur (Ed.), *How to recognize good policing: Problems and issues.* (pp. 55-72). Thousand Oaks, CalA: Sage.

Reisberg, L. (2000, August 11). A Professor's Controversial Analysis of Why Black Students Are Losing the Race: Berkeley scholar says their own anti-intellectualism prevents academic success. The Chronicle of Higher Education. A51. [On-Line], Available: http;//

Ritzer, G. (1993). *The McDonaldization of society. An investigation into the changing character of contemporary social life.* Thousand Oaks, CA: Pine Forge Press.

Roeber J & Ranalli, R 2000, August 17). 15 arrested, 1Mil in cocaine seized. B2.

Sacco, V.F. (1998). Evaluating satisfaction. In Jean-Paul Brodeur (Ed.), *How to recognize good policing: Problems and issues.* (pp. 123-140). Thousand Oaks, CA: Sage.

Sadd, S., & Grinc, R. (1994). Innovative neighborhood oriented policing: An evaluation of community policing programs in eight cities. In D.P. Rosenbaum (Ed.), *The challenge of community policing: Testing the promises* (pp. 27-52). Newbury Park, CA: Sage.

Schmalleger, F. (1999). *Criminology Today.* Upper Saddle River, NJ: Prentice Hall.

Sekulic, D., Massey, G, & Hodson, R. (1994). Who were the Yugoslavs? Failed sources of common identity in the former Yugoslavia. *American Sociological Review, 59*(1), 83-97.

Skogan, W.G. (1990). *Disorder and decline: Crime and the spiral of decay in American Neighborhoods.* NY: The Free Press.

Skogan, W.G. (1998). Community participation and community policing. In Jean-Paul Brodeur (Ed.), *How to recognize good policing: Problems and issues.* (pp. 88-106). Thousand Oaks, CA: Sage.

Sherman, LW. (1995). The police. In James Q. Wilson and Joan Petersilia (EDS.), *Crime.* (pp.327-348). San Francisco: Institute for Contemporary Studies.

Stephens, D.W. (1996). *Community problem oriented policing: Measuring impact, quantifying quality in policing.* Washington DC: Police Executive Research Forum.

Stevens, D.J. (2002a). *Case Studies in Community Policing.* Upper Saddle River, NJ: Prentice Hall.

(2002b). *Policing and Community Partnerships.* (Editor). Upper Saddle River, NJ: Prentice Hall.

(2002c). The threat of civil liabilities and probable cause arrests. The Police Journal. In press.

(2001). A study of three generations of incarcerated sexual offenders. Journal of Policing and Criminal Psychology.

(2001b). Police management styles and community policing and TQM. Community Policing Consortium. U.S. Department of Justice. Office of Community Oriented Policing Studies.

(2000) Identifying criminal predators, sentences, and criminal classifications. *Journal of Police and Criminal Psychology.* Spring.

(1999a) Do college educated officers provide quality police service? *Law and Order.* December, 47(12), 37-41.

(1999b) Corruption Among narcotic Officers: A study of innocence and integrity. *Journal of Police and Criminal Psychology.* Fall, 14(2), 1-11.

(1999c) American police resolutions. *Police Journal*, LXXII(2). 140-150.

(1999d, September) Police officer stress. *Law and Order.* http://www.lawandordermag.com/index2.html

(1999e, March). Police tactical units and community response. *Law and Order.* 47(3), 48-52.

(1998). *Inside the mind of the serial rapist.* Bethesda, MD: Austin & Winfield Publishers.
http://www.amazon.com/exec/obidos/ASIN/1572921293/002-5756676-8984421

(1997). Influences of early childhood experiences on subsequent criminology violent behaviour. *Studies on Crime and Crime Prevention,* 6(1), 34-50.

Surveys of citizens attitudes. (1995). Telemasp Bulletin. Huntsville, Texas: Texas Law Enforcement Management and Administrative Problem, Bill Blackwood Enforcement Management Institute of Texas.

Thio, A. (2000). *Sociology: A Brief Introduction*. Boston: Allyn and Bacon.

Trojanowicz, R.C. (1982). *An evaluation of the neighborhood foot patrol program in Flint, Michigan*. East Lansing: Department of Criminal Justice, Michigan State University.

Trojanowicz, R.C., & Carter, D.L. (1988). *The philosophy and role of community policing*. East Lansing: National Neighborhood Foot Patrol Center, Michigan State University.

Trojanowicz, R.C., & Dixon, S.L. (1974). *Criminal justice and the community*. Englewood Cliffs, NJ: Prentice Hall.

Thurman, Q., & McGarrell, E.F. (1995, June). Findings of the 1994 Spokane Police Department Citizen Survey: Final report, Washington State Institute for Community Oriented Policing, Spokane, Washington.

Williams, M.R. (1985). *Neighborhood organizations: Seeds of a new urban life*. Westport, CN: Greenwood Press.

Wulff, D. (2000, January/February). Winning strategies offered for working with different cultures. *Community Policing Exchange, VII*(30), 1.

Click here to input the text of your references, if any. Entries should be listed alphabetically...each entry occurring on a separate line.)

ABOUT THE AUTHOR

Dr. Dennis J. Stevens has a Ph.D. from Loyola University of Chicago (1991) and is an Associate Professor of Criminal Justice at the College of Public and Community Service, University of Massachusetts Boston. In addition to teaching traditional and nontraditional students, he has taught, counseled, and lectured law enforcement officers at police academies and police stations such as the North Carolina Justice Academy. He has also taught and led group encounters among felons at maximum custody penitentiaries such as Attica in New York, Eastern and Women's Institute in North Carolina, Stateville and Joliet near Chicago, and CCI in Columbia, South Carolina. Currently, contracted through Boston University, Dr. Stevens instructs male and female felons at high custody prisons in Massachusetts and has conducted extensive profile assessments among sexual offenders, most recently child molesters. Additionally, he has facilitated many group encounters for a national nonprofit organization rendering assistance to parents in conflict with children. He has over sixty-five articles in national and international press on criminology, corrections, and policing. His books include *Perspective: Corrections* (Coursewise, 1997, editor), *Inside the Mind of the Serial Rapist* (Austin-Winfield, 1998), *Case Studies in Community Policing* (Prentice Hall, 2001), *Policing and Community Partnerships* (Prentice Hall, 2002), and two novels (available amazon.com). Currently, he is evaluating the community outreach of eight police departments across the county for a textbook on *Communities and Community Policing* contracted with Allyn and Bacon Publishers, Boston. Dr. Stevens can be reached at dennis.stevens@umb.edu

Appendix I

MADISON POLICE DEPARTMENT NEIGHBORHOOD SURVEY

Basic Interview Data

Neighborhood (Circle one):

- Your neighborhood is _____

Other: Street: _____

Perceptions of the Neighborhood:

- How long have you lived or worked in this neighborhood? Years _____ Months

- In general, in the past year, would you say this neighborhood has become a better place to live or a worse place to live, or stayed about the same (Circle Response).

    Better
    Worse
    About the Same
    Did not live here last year
    Don't know

- Now, I am going to read a list of things that you may think are current problems in this neighborhood. After I read each one, please tell me whether you think it is a big problem, some problem, or not a problem in this neighborhood. The first one is:

	Big Problem	Some	No	Don't Know
Litter and trash on the streets and sidewalks	1	2	3	4
Public drinking or gambling	1	2	3	4
Loud parties or noise	1	2	3	4
Bar time noise or disturbances	1	2	3	4
Illegal drug activity	1	2	3	4
Vandalism	1	2	3	4
Burglary	1	2	3	4
Robbery	1	2	3	4
Sexual Assault & Rape	1	2	3	4
Personal assault	1	2	3	4
Criminal Gang Activity	1	2	3	4
Aggressive panhandling/begging	1	2	3	4
Graffiti	1	2	3	4
Parking rules being ignored	1	2	3	4
Unsupervised juveniles/youth	1	2	3	4
Speeding and other moving traffic violations	1	2	3	4
Domestic Violence	1	2	3	4
Hate Crimes	1	2	3	4
Theft from Auto	1	2	3	4
Vandalism to Autos	1	2	3	4
Crimes Involving Firearms	1	2	3	4
Unsafe-Pedestrian/School Crossings	1	2	3	4

4. Do you feel there are other problems not listed. Yes No If yes, what are they?

5. In general, how safe do you feel out alone in this neighborhood. Do you feel:

   Very safe
   Somewhat safe
   Somewhat unsafe
   Very unsafe
   Don't know

6. In the past year, have you called the police to report a crime or problem that happened?

   Yes   How many times?
   No (skip to #8).

7. How satisfied were you with how the police handled this call? Would you say you were:

   Very satisfied
   Somewhat satisfied
   Somewhat dissatisfied
   Very dissatisfied
   Don't know

8. In general, how effective has MPD been in responding to problems and concerns in this neighborhood? Are they:

> Very effective
> Somewhat effective
> Somewhat ineffective
> Very ineffective
> Don't know

9. In general, do you feel police officers in this area treat people:

> Very reasonably
> Somewhat reasonably
> Somewhat unreasonably
> Very unreasonably
> Not sure

Community Involvement

10. How willing are area residents to work with police addressing problems here in the neighborhood?

> Very willing
> Somewhat willing
> Somewhat unwilling
> Very unwilling
> Don't know

11. Please indicate how strongly you agree or disagree with the following statements:

	Strongly Agree	Somewhat Agree	Somewhat Disagree	Strongly Disagree
Police officers should spend more time making personal contacts with neighborhood residents & businesses	4	3	2	1
Police officers should be assigned to a neighborhood on a long-term basis	4	3	2	1
I would like to see officers more involved in community programs such as school activities	4	3	2	1
I feel comfortable contacting the Police Department to make suggestions or complaints against its employees	4	3	2	1
Making communities safer and more livable is a responsibility that should be shared by both the police and community residents	4	3	2	1
I would like to be informed of community policing activities in my neighborhood.	4	3	2	1

Perceptions of Police, City Services and Other Programs

12. All things considered, do you think the neighborhood a year from now will be a:

> Better place to live
> Stay about the same
> Become somewhat worse
> Not sure

13. Rate your level of satisfaction with the Madison Police Department in the following areas:

	Very Satisfied	Somewhat Satisfied	Somewhat Dissatisfied	Very Dissat
Providing quick response to emergency situations	4	3	2	1
Controlling crime in your Neighborhood	4	3	2	1
Helping with neighborhood Nuisance problems	4	3	2	1
Providing crime prevention advice	4	3	2	1
Understanding community Concerns	4	3	2	1
Providing fair and equal Treatment to all	4	3	2	1
Addressing traffic problems	4	3	2	1

14. Calls for service which are not emergencies can often be handled by alternative, non-conventional methods. Please indicate whether or not the following options would be acceptable to you:

	Yes	No
The officer schedules an appointment to meet you at a later time	____	____
The report is handled over the telephone		
You fill out a report from and mail it to the Police Department		
You fill out a report and fax it to the Police Department		
The report is made in person at the police facility		
A report could be filed to the department through the Internet		

15. Do you have anything to add?

_____

16. Finally, I would like to ask a few general questions about you. In which category do you fit?

How old are you? _____

17. Which of these apply to you?

I own a residence (home) here in the neighborhood
I reside in an apartment in the neighborhood
I work or volunteer here in the neighborhood
I work in or own a business in the neighborhood

18. What is your racial or ethnic identity? Are you:

African American
White
Hispanic
Asian/Pacific Islander
American Indian
Something Else
No Answer

Appendix II

Do not write your name on this survey. It's confidential. Your survey will be seen only by the researcher: Dennis J. Stevens, University of Massachusetts Boston who is evaluating the promises of the police through their community policing efforts. Your input will be compared with other residents to better understand your experiences and your needs. Feel free to mail this survey to me or if you have any questions about it I can be reached at: dennis.stevens@umb.edu: or my address is UMB, 100 Morrissey Blvd. Boston, MA 02125-3393. Thanks.

1. What is the name of the neighborhood and the city you live?

(neighborhood) _____ (city) _____

2. How long have you lived in this neighborhood? _____

3. Would you briefly describe your occupation? _____

4. In the past year, has your neighborhood become: (Check One Only)

   A much safer place to live _____
   A safe place to live _____
   About the same _____

An unsafe place to live   _____
A very unsafe place   _____

5. If you've had contact with the police in the last year, what was the nature of some of those of those contacts?

I reported an accident _____ or a crime _____
I was arrested _____
I was the victim of a crime _____
I was issued a citation _____
I was a witness to a crime _____
I was in a motor vehicle accident _____
I was contacted about a problem or disturbance _____
I requested information _____
I attended community policing meetings _____ (where) _____
I was involved in another way with the department (please specify) ____

6. Overall, how would you rate the performance of the officers involved?
Professional ____ Fair ____ Frightening ____ Intimidating ____
If you've remembered their names, please list: _____

7. Based on your contact with police at a crime scene, rate the following:

Item	Excellent	Good	Fair	Poor	Very Poor
Response Time					
Solved the Problem					
Made me Feel Comfortable					
Helpfulness					
Dress/Appearance					

8. How often do community members help the department make decisions about:

Item	Always	Very Often	Often	Sel-dom	Never
Routine Police Auto Patrol	5	4	3	2	1
Routine Bike/Boat Patrol	5	4	3	2	1
Decisions at Mini Stations	5	4	3	2	1
Building Owner Notification	5	4	3	2	1
Use of Police Force	5	4	3	2	1
Priorities of Calls for Service	5	4	3	2	1
Police Officer Disciplinary Actions	5	4	3	2	1
Police Training Courses	5	4	3	2	1
Officer Promotion Committees	5	4	3	2	1

10. How willing are the residents in your community to work with police addressing problems in the neighborhood?

Very willing _____
Somewhat willing _____
Somewhat unwilling _____
Very unwilling _____
Don't know _____
Community members have their own agenda _____

11. In general, how effective has the department been in responding to problems in your neighborhood? Are they:

Very effective _____
Somewhat effective _____
Somewhat ineffective _____
Very ineffective _____
Don't know _____
The police have their own agenda _____

12. Please indicate how strongly you agree or disagree with the following statements:

	Strongly Agree	Some-what Agree	Some-what Disagree	Strongly Disagree	Not Sure
Police officers should spend more time making personal contacts with neighborhood residents and businesses	5	4	3	2	1
Police officers should be assigned to a neighborhood on a long-term basis	5	4	3	2	1
I would like to see officers more involved in community programs such as school activities	5	4	3	2	1

At community meetings, police talk down to us.	5	4	3	2	1
The police listen to our non-criminal concerns and act upon them.	5	4	3	2	1
I feel comfortable contacting the Police Department to make suggestions or complaints against their personnel	5	4	3	2	1
Making communities safer is a responsibility that should be shared by police, community residents, and business operators	5	4	3	2	1

13. All things considered, do you think the neighborhood a year from now will:

    Be a better place to live _____
    Stay about the same _____
    Become worse _____
    Not sure _____

14. I would like to ask a few general questions about you and your ideas.

    How old are you? _____

15. Do you own _____ rent _____ your residents or live with someone _____?

16. In a single word, how would you describe your race?

    _____

17. Which country do you consider to be your homeland?

    _____

18. Your Gender:

    Male   _____
    Female _____

19. What language is usually spoken at home? _____

20. Identify the 3 biggest problems that need to be addressed in your community?

    _____
    _____
    _____
    _____

21. In your opinion, what actions should be taken to curb the 3 biggest problems in your community?

_____

_____

_____

_____

22. At community meetings, do folks usually work together?

Most of the time ____ Some of the time ____ Seldom ____ Never ____

23. Would you say that everybody (i.e. elderly, youth, former offenders) in the community is encouraged to attend community meetings?

Most of the time ____ Some of the time ____ Seldom ____ Never ____

24. How often do community members leave meetings with mental "to do" lists?

Always ____ Very Often ____ Sometimes ____ Seldom ____ Never ____

25. How often are the actions to resolve community problems actually developed by the community members?

Always ____ Very Often ____ Sometimes ____ Seldom ____ Never ____

26. How often are police actions talked about at meetings?

Always ____ Very Often ____ Sometimes ____ Seldom ____ Never ____

27. How often are those actions changed to fit the results?

Always _____ Very Often _____ Sometimes _____ Seldom _____ Never _____

28. Would you say the plans made at community meetings concerning crime control is generally:

Practical _____ Impractical _____ Not Sure _____

29. In what way is the community safer since the community started meeting?

_____

30. In what way have the police contributed to a safer community?

_____

NOTES

i   Available on-line at web site: http://www.fbi.gov/ucr.htm

ii   For an indepth discussion on cause and effect relationships, see Dean Champion (1993).

iii   Variables refer to any phenomena that can assume more than one value. Establishing cause and outcome relationships between variables also suggests that the cause or independent variable is antecedent (prior) in time to the outcome.

iv   See the New York Times, June 22, 1982, p. C2.

v   Some people like to refer to a causal question as a hypothesis.

vi   Note: This Introduction complete with its citations and references is a similar introduction that other investigators are expected to develop.

vii   The police agencies evaluated were Broken Arrow, OK; Camden, NJ: Columbus, OH; Fayetteville, NC; Harris County, Precinct 4, TX; Lansing, MI; Nashville, TN; Sacramento, CA; and St. Petersburg, FL. This is the same study that was presented earlier in this chapter and in Table 1-4. Some of these agencies did little to professionally evaluate their community policing initiatives and as one result, failed often. For some of these agencies that failed, little could have saved them since there were many factors deterring a community policing philosophy. Yet it was believed that those agencies might have been better prepared for their failure had they exercised a professional methodological system to aid them in understanding where the pit falls were within their city government among their community members prior to initiating a community policing policy (Stevens, 2002a).

viii For a closer look at these ideas see David L. Carter and Louis A. Radelet, (2000). The police and the community. Upper Saddle River, NJ: Prentice Hall.

ix The University of Wisconsin is the home of retired professor emeritus and one of the architects of community policing, Herman Goldstein.

x Captain Michael F. Masterson provided the leadership for the Madison Police Department to develop, conduct, and evaluate their community policing initiatives. In the interest of sharing information so others may learn, Captain Masterson routinely writes about contemporary police issues, in this case Madison's success of measuring community policing performance.

xi The Stage presentation was inspired by Popenoe (2000). Many of the definitions were borrowed from Champion (1993) and Thio (2000). However, most of what is written about testing performance fits into years of experience of training police officers, correctional officers, and other students including incarcerated felons on how to conduct an explicit test.

xii Community policing philosophy includes among other things community member participation in police decisions.

xiii Articles containing investigations comprised of similar guidelines that follow the five Stages discussed in this section - that is, a media review (problem formulation), test design and sample, collect and process data, results (findings), and analysis of those results (conclusion) or what some writers call an empirical study).

xiv It is strongly suggested that before you write your narrative, you create your reference page containing all of your references and then (on another page) write a short paragraph explaining how each reference is linked to your causal relationship. These simple steps will save you a great deal of energy when you're developing your problem formulation narrative. Also, this method will aid in organization of your work and help you stay on target.

xv Are you measuring what you think you're measuring?

xvi Try to follow this advise in interviews too for more valid results.

xvii See Stevens (2000).

xviii For more detail see Dean Champion (1993). There are four types of validity. Content validity refers to the logical conclusions of a sampling of items taken from the universe or items that measure the trait in question. Predictive validity is based on the measured association between what an instrument predicts behavior will be and the subsequent behavior exhibited by an individual. Concurrent validity is closely connected to predictive validity but differs in that the scores are obtained simultaneously with the exhibited behavior. And lastly, construct validity is both a logical and a statistical validating method.

xix See: Publication Manual of the American Psychological Association, 4th edition ISBN 55-798-241-4. $21.95. (Spanish Edition Available). Available on-line at www.apa.org. Also, recommended is: Mastering APA Style: Student Workbook and Training Guide. ISBN 1-55798-085-3. Cost. $19.95. Available www.apa.org.